AND THE WALLS CAME
TUMBLING DOWN

AND THE WALLS CAME TUMBLING DOWN

40 Encouragements to Elevate the Mind in the Midst of a Storm, Based on Real-Life Experiences

JAHMELLA ROBINSON

To order additional copies of this book, contact:
Xlibris
1-888-795-4274
www.Xlibris.com
Orders@Xlibris.com
784240

TABLE OF CONTENTS

Dedication

This book is dedicated to everyone who needs encouragement to own their story. Every trial, tribulation and flaw will be overcome for God's glory.

Preface

Many may enquire why I would openly share my journey of growth. I'm convinced there is much power in testifying of God's power at work in each of us. By this, I'm referring to sanctification. The Holy Spirit residing within us moulds us over time to the likeness of our Lord and Saviour. Why hide this? Why rob God of His glory? As people enslaved by Christ for His glory, we should do everything to give Him glory (1 Corinthians 7:22), including living openly in the absence of a façade. There is healing in being vulnerable, and we overcome by the power of our testimony (Revelation 12:11). We are relatable when we reveal our human side—yes, our flaws—and the positive change we and others witness over time. It is very empowering. Salvation is not because of anything we've done, so let's continue to keep it real (Ephesians 2:8-9).

2 Corinthians 12:19 (NIV) says: "But he said to me, 'My grace is sufficient for you, for my power is made perfect in weakness.' Therefore I will boast all the more gladly about my weaknesses, so that Christ's power may rest on me." I completely embrace this verse!

I hope we never feel the need to put up a façade of perfection. Let's not be modern-day Pharisees; confession is necessary for cleansing (1 John 1:9). If we don't yet have one or two non-judgemental partners for accountability, I strongly recommend we get this. It is important to examine self, but remember:

while we can take steps to rectify our flaws based on willpower, it is in Him where we find rest for our weary souls. He is the potter and we are the clay (Isaiah 64:8, Romans 9:21).

When we abide in Him (John 15:1-4), things always fall into place for the better—that is our thoughts, behaviours, and characteristics change over time to honour Him. Be patient with self and others, as it can take weeks, months, or even years, but the breakthrough will come.

If people around us choose not to endure us as we go through the process of pruning, that's not really something we can control. A sister in Christ reminded me that it can reveal the status of their hearts, as we all need to exercise patience with each other as we are all moulded towards Christ. I'm very mindful of destiny helpers and destiny anchors in life. This consciousness has resulted in not only my spiritual growth, but me being catapulted into my purpose. I pray this book blesses you immensely.

Acknowledgement

I thank the Lord first and foremost for hearing my cry back on December 31st, 2016, when it all could have ended. I thank Him for giving me divine instruction and the strength to be obedient.

I thank my mum for encouraging me to share my story in the form of a book. I thank my family for tolerating me over the years, so much so that I have never felt uncomfortable to admit my flaws and to be patient with growth areas.

I thank the 'Encouragers'—you know who you are—for your continued support and for pushing me to get this assignment completed on God's schedule, not mine. I thank each and every recipient of the encouraging messages I've sent weekly or fortnightly over the last five years or so. Your expression of gratitude and communication of relevance and impact have spurred me on.

CHAPTER 1: THE FOUNDATIONS

Bastian: "Why is it so dark?"
Empress Moonchild: "In the beginning it is always dark"

The NeverEnding Story *movie quote*

Early Years

It started out in a two-bedroom flat in Camberwell, in South East London, with four siblings and me in one room, parents in the other. I remember my brothers on a bunk bed and my two sisters and me on a fold-up single bed. Yes, you read that correctly: three in a single bed! I remember watching the Power Rangers series on Saturday mornings, and playing out with the neighbours' kids. I can't forget my aunty and cousin who lived one floor above. The good old days. Everyone knew everyone. Community spirit at its best.

We all start from the bottom—reminds me of Zechariah 4:10

I attended a nursery in Camberwell for a brief time in which I had one friend called Joe—English kid, if I recall. Classmates were neighbours in the same flat—one big happy community. Apparently, when my older sister pushed me down the ramp outside the flat when I was on a skateboard, my older cousin, in my defence, hit my older sister's head against the brick wall as punishment. I'd like to believe this is somewhat of an exaggeration, created from a young mind who recalls details of events inaccurately given it took place over two decades ago. Older sis, I'm so sorry.

The importance of community in shaping the young; feeling safe and settled—reminds me of Psalm 91:1

The First Move

We moved to good old Peckham, to the infamous Acorn Estate. Another estate which became well known as 'Yellow Brick' was the rival; apparently it was a lot more dangerous. I shared a bedroom with my two sisters, my brothers shared a room, and our parents were in the other. The fourth bedroom, which became known as the 'little room', was linked to the balcony. It was mainly used for storage; while there was a bed in it, there was also a load of junk—items one did not want to throw away but did not have use for. I suppose my dad could have been considered somewhat of a hoarder back then. It was pretty cramped, but we made do.

Mi Familia

My older brothers were always around. The eldest was into sports coaching and the next one into contemporary dance. Promising futures were ahead of them, but life caused several stumbling blocks. When my eldest brother was chased up a block of flats by a group of young guys who thought they were 'too cool for school', he had no choice but to jump down the front of the stairs for his survival and limp home. With a damaged knee and months of physiotherapy, his sports coaching career became a distant memory. This didn't affect his provider mentality; he's happily married with a beautiful family which is still growing.

This type of experience was not a rarity for either of my brothers, unfortunately. My brothers both had baseball bats in their rooms going forward, for safety. My second brother was fond of the arts; contemporary dance was his thing, and he performed so passionately at the BRIT School for Performing Arts & Technology. Keen on the ladies and sometimes distracted, he found his new strength in the gift of the gab—sales. He loved the game of monopoly, and opened his own estate agent. This goes to show that childhood ambitions can manifest.

My older sister was reading at two years old and able to write beautiful poetry from a young age. It's a shame she didn't achieve the A grade she deserved at school due to incompetent teachers consistently losing her coursework. No, the system is not fair. But this might have been part of a bigger plan because my older sister selflessly supported and cared for the elderly with mental health challenges.

My younger sister was the sweetest thing I had ever seen. I felt bad when her academic development slowed due to my dad working long hours, and my mum working two jobs day and night. As siblings we happily rallied together to teach her how to tell time, and to read, but I do believe it to be unacceptable for siblings to take on the responsibility of raising each other. Parents get busy or lazy, and siblings pay the price. Sis, I'm sorry you didn't get the same daily homeschooling we received when we were your age. Bills had to be paid. Nevertheless, my younger sister went on to achieve big. She not only decided to support toddlers in their development, but she performed in the theatre too.

Now that I think about it, it's fair to say that our house was overcrowded; however, I didn't see this at the time. Surely it was the norm to receive hand-me-down clothes, and trainers valued at £2 from LidL—I still recall the grey and green design. Yes, comments were made during PE classes, but it didn't knock my confidence as I wasn't alone; I knew my older sister was in a similar pair. If she could wear them, then so could I. Kids can be so cruel, but there was no better opportunity to develop thick skin, and to begin to feel set apart from the norm.

I'm quite sure my half-brother would visit on weekends once a month, and stay in the 'little room'. I'm sure his pillow always smelt like cherries after he had left. Or was it my mind playing tricks on me, clinging to his desired presence, making up preferred smells to ensure his presence lingered?

I wouldn't say my mum was a traditional housewife given that she worked two jobs. She worked in our primary school during the day—always a pleasure seeing her in the playground!—and within the catering industry during the evenings. However, she still managed to make most of our clothes—correction: some of our clothes. Very talented lady. She baked bread rolls for my dad to take to work each day and provided him with his daily portion of fruits. She cooked dinner every day before her evening shift too—super woman!

My dad worked an unskilled labour job, driving a forklift for over thirty years in a paper factory. He used to listen to the audio Bible while working all of those hours—safe to say he's well versed in the Word of God! He was persecuted daily for his faith; he was a man of integrity and always worked as if he was working for the Lord. Naturally, colleagues of a lazy disposition did not like this, so he became an easy target. He always had a witty response to the foolish arguments and accusations brought before him. Thirty years of hardship. My dad can testify to long suffering and endurance. The main impact of this was fatigue in the evenings. He was also very passionate about the Bible, so much so that it was all he could talk about, in the evenings after work and all day on the weekends. I salute his passion for the faith, and we were given a solid foundation in biblical theology as a result.

We honoured the Sabbath, the seventh day of the week, Saturday, and kept it holy in the sense that no one worked on

Saturday and dinner was cooked by my mum the day before. There was even a weekly fast from TV on Saturdays to encourage 'family time', which consisted of sleeping in until perhaps 11.00 a.m., waking up to the sounds of Premier Christian radio, and to the smell of plantain, scrambled eggs and bakes.

The importance of resting for at least one day a week—reminds me of Exodus 20:8

Kid's Company

"Problems, problems, problems, problems, should I go to school? Or should I stay at home, pretending I'm sickly, locked up in my room?" The lyrics to a song written by the group as a collective. We were very young, under eight even. This charity supported us, as disadvantaged children, and guided us towards teamwork and community spirit. Who wouldn't have minded performing on stage and being filmed by channel 4? Even if we just mouthed the words rather than actually allowing our beautiful voices to be heard.

Play Time

We used to 'play out' in the 'square' on the estate. Oh the joys of being young and carefree. Occasionally, we would take trips to the park around the corner. It was the place to be on weekends: swings, slide, rocking horse. We often sought permission to play in the front garden; I can never forget that we were blessed to have our own personal source of oxygen freely flowing towards our house, our own gigantic tree that the council refused to cut down. I preferred our back garden, however; it had a pond I was rather fond of—RIP Kermit the frog one and Kermit the frog two. The neighbour's cat Felix will get what's coming to him, if he hasn't already.

When my dad purchased my mum and younger sister new bikes, they were very happy! Until within forty-eight hours they were nicked from the back garden. Good old safe Peckham. It turns out the perpetrators climbed into the back garden, unlocked the back gate, stole the bikes, jumped back into the back garden, locked the gate—thanks for that!—then fled the crime scene. Of course the incident wasn't reported to the police. What would've been the realistic expected outcome given the absence of cameras? It was pre-2000, after all.

Riding our BMX bikes was a good pastime. I'm still unsure as to how we came to have the bikes. Mine was red and brown, whilst my older sister's was light blue. I believe my dad may have found the bikes out back in the rubbish and fixed them up; he was always handy with chains and things. I enjoyed riding the bikes through the back alleyway, where full bin bags were stored, ready for collection. I wouldn't encourage any child to pursue such an area for leisure activities; however, when young, one doesn't notice that they're playing near a dump despite the flies being a strong giveaway. Such innocence. Such ignorance.

The beauty of our carefree youth—reminds me of Matthew 19:14

I remember playing knock down ginger and 40-40 home, as well as conkers, and just walking in the woodchip area, which was rumoured to have horse manure in it. It was always fun when our older cousin came to visit, often with a school friend or two, or a new boyfriend. I think at least two were called Ricky! Crop tops were the in thing during those years, based off my cousin's choice of clothing; she always looked so trendy! It was a joy when my cousin brought us hand-me-down clothes, as they were often saucy in nature and naturally, while we were allowed to wear them, this permission was restricted to within our house only.

My dearest cousin would take us to the shop to get penny sweets. These were sweets commercially valued at one penny. Twenty pennies' worth was heaven, and fifty pennies' worth was paradise. Strawberries and bananas were my favourite, valued at two pennies each, along with sugary strawberry laces at half the price of the other two.

Bert's Sweet Shop was one door down from the local chippy; for the decade that we lived there, I only entered that chip shop once. It seemed Netto's chips were more cost effective. The appearance of the ice cream van was the precipice of my glorious summer holidays. However, this was a rarity. Again, it seemed that Netto's Cornish ice cream was more cost effective. Or choc ice. We seemed to shop everywhere, wherever the deal was. Oh the life of a young'un with four siblings.

The humble life is the best life—reminds me of Luke 14:28-30

The community came together when Bert's wife passed away. His grandson took over the shop. My brothers attended the funeral. Suddenly the things I took comfort in, my norm, were changing rather rapidly. When one of my dad's cousins died, there was sadness in the family. When one of my mum's good friends died, there was sadness in the family.

Death is a natural part of life; use it for empowerment rather than discouragement—reminds me of Ecclesiastes 3:2

Non-Stop Box

Christmas must have arrived early the evening my dad came home with a car full of surprise boxes. Slight joke because anyone who knows us knows we don't celebrate Christmas. It was deemed pagan by the head of the house, my dad, and so we honoured him by being compliant—as if we had a choice, eh?

When my dad arrived home, he had seven big boxes, brown in colour and very easy to open. I couldn't contain my excitement. When I ripped off the brown Sellotape, I was able to see the contents of my box. On the top were many bags of Walkers crisps. I say Walkers, but really it was unbranded Netto crisps. It didn't matter as long as the prawn cocktail flavour was there, and it was. We don't eat pork. We weren't allowed to eat from any animal that parts the hoof or chews the cud. No pigs. No gelatine. No prawns, no shrimp. It was a miracle we were allowed to eat prawn cocktail-flavoured crisps. It felt like we had permission to rebel. I remember eating salt and vinegar crisps that evening, and the crisp was so sharp it cut my cheek. We became enemies. Never again did I eat salt and vinegar crisps... until adulthood.

Beneath the crisps were chocolates. Beneath the chocolates were Non-Stop boxes. Non-Stop boxes were small square soft mints. They were the bomb diggity. My dad used to bring a few packets home each week as a treat, so to be presented with a big brown box of them was literally a dream come true. It is by God's grace alone that we aren't victims to diabetes considering the way we devoured the chocolates and Non-Stop boxes. Once it was gone, it was gone. We learnt to manage our treat. We learnt that good things can come to an end. We learnt that if we chose to overconsume, resulting in stomach pain or skin breakouts, we only had ourselves to blame.

Rationing

Have you ever faced that annoying situation where you go to use a bathroom to discover, too late, that the toilet roll is finished? My dad is full of clever ideas and wanted to get to the bottom of the matter. We were given nine rolls each, and if we went to the loo and forgot ours, we'd borrow from each other and pay back in loo roll sheets. We quickly learned to not be overgenerous with the tissue. Interesting strategy for encouraging behavioural change—I mean, it was genius even. The desired outcome was reached. It wasn't me.

Honeysuckle Tree

We used to eat trees. No, no, no, don't let your imagination run wild! No herbs. The honeysuckle tree has an unusual composition, such that if you pull off the flower and remove the green part at the bottom, a very sweet juice oozes out. For many years, this satisfied our sugar cravings while we played out in the front garden. The tree was actually in the neighbour's garden, and the common understanding was that we were free to pick away. Generous.

The Neighbourhood

There was only one other Bajan household in the 'square'. For those who may be unaware, Bajan refers to people from the beautiful island of Barbados. The other Bajan family bought a black cat named Pebbles, and when Pebbles had many kittens, there was huge excitement in the 'square'. My favourite was Jazz. Jazz was a male. He was strong-willed and pleasant to stroke. I used to put milk in one of the breakfast bowls from the kitchen and leave it out in the garden. My mum wasn't pleased, but Jazz was happy, and that was all that mattered to me at the time. Despite this experience, I remain convinced that I could never have a cat. To be responsible for the life of a little feline seemed too heavy a burden. Plus, my parents would never allow it. I know, because I asked several times.

There was a rather unusual gentleman in the tower block to the left of our houses. He seemed friendly enough, but was unusual because he often fed kids dog biscuits as a treat. I don't recall seeing his dog, ever, but he must've had one since he had dog biscuits, right? He was known to curse a lot, and one of his hands had only three fingers. As a child, I remembered this.

Protect the ears of the young; teach them what is acceptable— reminds me of Proverbs 22:6

The neighbours to the right of us were a lovely Columbian family. There was a mum, a dad, five kids and a female dog. One evening, my mum braided their daughter's hair for school photo day; it was later reported that the neighbour's daughter was egged by a few boys who fancied her. I'm sure she would've much appreciated a simple conversation; however, boys will be boys.

The neighbour to the left of us was an elderly Jamaican lady. She was a sweetheart. We used to play out with her grandchildren in our front gardens. She required respect from all. Great lady. Great family.

NAGTY

I was identified as being eligible for the National Academy of Gifted and Talented Youth; this was founded in 2002 and was around for about five years. Only high-achieving Secondary students in England were considered for this initiative - the top 5% to be correct. The extra-curricular activities on offer were amazing! One summer, I spent two weeks on a course at Imperial College in London and met some really cool people. We were tasked with creating a robot and presenting our findings in a Dragon's Den type of setting. Olivia was a fictional robotic window cleaner – we came in third place. There was the usual coupling up, as there always is at these summer courses, at that age. We all went to the BBC Proms a couple of times, the V&A museum, and local parks. We even had an end-of-course party;

I must confess though that getting told off for 'dropping it like it was hot' was a secret highlight of the night. Fun times!

The Second Move

We moved from Peckham to Peckham. Accomplishment! This house was bigger and better. No front garden, smaller back garden but bigger rooms. The structure of this house stood out to me, namely that the living room was on the first floor, and I had never seen such before. Big brother in one room, me and younger sis in another, and older sis finally in her own room. I know she was happy. We were all happy.

Love Thyself

There is something seriously wrong with not feeling content in one's own skin. I'm reminded of the chorus of the song "Unpretty" sung by the group TLC. Fortunately for me, not only does my Heavenly Father convince me that I am beautifully and wonderfully made in His image, but my dad has always been very bold in his stance that his daughters are beautiful.

Yes, when we were younger, we missed out on experimenting with makeup, nail polish, jewellery, etc., but we felt and feel secure enough not to rely on these things to enhance our already existing beauty, or to somehow validate ourselves with external additions.

If I had a pound for every time a female, usually of ethnic minority origin, would blurt out, "Have you considered weave?" It makes me sad, genuinely, that even if my hair is tidied and styled in a socially acceptable way, due to brainwashing, these ladies can't identify with the beauty in its plain and simple form. For the hundredth time, if it doesn't come out of my scalp,

I'm not wearing it. Each to their own, or '*lef mi be nah*', as they say in Jamaica.

During the teenage years, I noticed I had put on a few extra pounds. It could've been due to one too many Snickers bars, or was it Maltesers? My older sister had also gone through a podgy phase, and I knew it was pending for my younger sister. It's so easy to think less of oneself when weight is gained. My dad was on hand to encourage us, to restore our initial belief that we were beautiful. He'd reaffirm us and tell us we needed the extra pounds in case we became ill, in which case if we lost our appetites, our body would have extra weight to feed on. Who would've thought the belly bulge could be considered beneficial? I consider it so important to hear from the head of the house that we had and have internal and external beauty.

The Family that Works Out Together Stays Together

There was a routine in place. Every evening, when my dad arrived home from work, we would exercise together as a family. The routine would last for about an hour. It consisted of a warm-up, cardio routine, then gymnastics, and then cool-down. It was a very good source of discipline for us in the evenings after school, and a great way to channel any excess energy. We loved star jumps, attempting the splits, and handstands against the wall.

It wasn't until recently that I reflected, and realised there was in fact a level of resentment towards the task. A whole sixty minutes was a long time to stay focused. We wouldn't dare complain. We fell in line. We stayed physically fit and rightly so.

Channel the excess energy in sport—reminds me of 1 Timothy 4:8

Primary School

Primary school was a blur. I remember dating a guy in year three who had four girlfriends in total at the same time; they were my closest female friends as well. All four relationships lasted for one week, and started and ended in the same week. They say players start young. I'd like to think he's a one-woman type of gentleman now.

I recall a certain Jamaican teacher who used to lay down the law in her classroom; I enjoyed her storybooks about Anansi the Spider. I strongly believe that having a Caribbean schoolteacher while having Caribbean heritage was a real blessing in a Western world, especially at that age.

Discipline is vital, and I recall a certain young man who was told to stand on the table due to poor behaviour; the class was instructed to point at him and say, "Shame, shame, you know your name". Fun times for us. Sad times for him. Sorry, kid. I'm sure he learnt respect as a result.

Better to face embarrassment when young than when grown— reminds me of Hebrews 12:11

I was getting lippy to my mum. I had a habit of name-calling her and had developed a poor, disrespectful attitude. The talk at home was that I was 'overdue some beatings'. One evening after school, my time came and my dad, the strong disciplinarian, took the necessary action. I remember the pain, and the shame. I recall laughing at my mum one evening, and within seconds, it was time to be disciplined. In this instance, what hurt was having her boast about it to her good friend an hour later. Whilst I don't agree with such methods of discipline, methods which I have purposely not named, it's safe to say that the desired outcome was achieved in which I learned discipline.

Respect your elders—reminds me of Proverbs 23:13

Secondary School

I didn't get the position of student captain or a place on the student council—their loss. In order to obtain a leadership position, one needs confidence. I did not have confidence. My loss, really.

I never thought I was any good at art, yet I managed to find a loophole to secure an A grade. Just because the drawing didn't look like the subject, it didn't make the drawing any less acceptable; the secret was to annotate the artwork, to explain what could have been done differently to improve it. Somehow I achieved an A grade. My annotations must have been awesome.

I enjoyed maths, good old algebra, and the trampoline in PE. I can never forget when I received detention for lying about pushing my good friend down the stairs; no idea what I was thinking, and friend, I am still so sorry.

Always tell the truth. It will most definitely set you free— reminds me of John 8:32

I was known as a 'boffin' back then, always in my books. It was a good escape from the distraction of those my age constantly playing out. I didn't think I was better than them; I just wanted to succeed. A desire placed on my heart at a young age, to earn big, achieve big, change my circumstance. I was of a quiet disposition; this was frequently confirmed at parents' evenings. I knew this would have to change and that I'd have to speak up at college.

College

I was actually drawn to attend a different sixth form college to the one I ended up going to. I was drawn to the life of the college, but during the opening day, my mum caught sight of a couple making out and deemed the college to be 'too slack' for her daughter.

Most times, parents know best. Trust their experience and wisdom—reminds me of Job 12:12

I studied very academic subjects at college, receiving A levels in maths, history and economics. I completed an AS level in politics. Despite enjoying politics, I chose to drop this subject and kept maths instead—maths being my weaker subject, but one I would need to get into the university course I had in mind. With hindsight, I wish I had stuck with what I was good at, and at that which I enjoyed, rather than choosing the subject that would get me to the career I thought I wanted in order to have money that I thought I wanted. Funnily enough, the majority of my economics class chose to study economics at university; our teacher was ace, intelligent and witty.

It was time to come out of my shell. I ran for student president, and with tears in my eyes I gave my speech, as my partner had left me to it on the day. A good friend at the time stood next to me as I powerfully stated my case for the presidency. Needless to say, I lost, but I was well known for months to come and easily secured my position on the student council. That was good enough for me.

At last I had found my confidence, and it felt as if I could do and be anything, equal to every man, able to achieve anything I desired and worked towards.

University

I secured a place in my first-choice school, making me the first in the family to go to university. Luckily my dad agreed to cover my tuition, which meant I only needed the maintenance loan—thanks, older sis, for your efforts in driving this arrangement.

When I began university, I had the mindset of a leader and wanted responsibility from day one. When I was encouraged to be considered for Student Representative for Economics, I knew my journey was just beginning. As the hunger to stretch myself grew, I took on additional responsibilities. With the support of the previous role holder, I was voted to be the Finance Officer of the African Caribbean and Asian Society, rescuing the society from an unfortunate negative balance due to unforeseen circumstances at the time. I coordinated with course mates and set up the first Business, Management and Economics Society that the university had ever had. Whilst it was hard to maintain since we missed the boat for sponsorships, it was still a good effort by those involved.

The move to university was a struggle for my younger sister, and whilst she didn't communicate this to me, as she didn't bother to call me, I was made aware from my mum that she would often put the two single beds together and sleep in one big bed, on my side, as she missed me. Had I known, I would've visited home more often.

I only really went home to do laundry or to raid the fridge.

Think of others always—reminds me of Philippians 2:4

Since both brothers had moved out, each of us ladies had our own room. Somebody shout, "Freedom!" Three years away for university is a long time. It seemed to be a time to be selfish, and to enjoy life with friendships, relationships, nights out. I did get stuck into ministry, after God removed a distraction.

Final year exams were terrifying. Something went terribly wrong with one of our papers, such that a draft version of the question sheet was presented to each student. Thankfully, this was rectified and did not negatively impact our overall degree grades. In the moment, it was truly frightening, and I regret not submitting this fear to God at the time. Funnily enough, all things worked out either way.

There is never really a need to worry because everything works out in the end—reminds me of Matthew 6:25-34.

CHAPTER 2: THE WORKMAN IS WORTHY OF HIS MEAT

"The world ain't all sunshine and rainbows. It is a very mean and nasty place and it will beat you to your knees and keep you there permanently if you let it. You, me, or nobody is gonna hit as hard as life. But it ain't how hard you hit; it's about how hard you can get hit, and keep moving forward. How much you can take, and keep moving forward. That's how winning is done."

Rocky Balboa *movie quote*

Career Foundation

Our washing machine broke down. It must've been God ordained. My mum kept a book detailing the dates we used the new washing machine and how much we saved each time by not spending money at the laundrette. Who would've thought this would lay the foundation of my professional career? I wanted to be an accountant, thinking that was where the money was. My dad's best friend was an accountant for Tesco at the time. I had it all planned: after early retirement as an accountant, I'd be an Art Teacher. Those were my plans, but God had other plans.

Start Early

Let's take a step back in time. Just after secondary school, I secured my first internship at an American investment bank. At age sixteen, it felt amazing to get my first suit, my first set of work heels. I thought I really looked the part with my chequered sleeveless sweater. Let's keep it our little secret that my clothes were purchased from the infamous Primark.

I loved every minute of being at the firm. The biggest shock to me was that every single employee I met was super passionate about their role. A South African lady stood out to me; she absolutely loved her job. I wanted to be her! She explained that if she worked late, the firm would cover the cost of the taxi to take her home. This blew my young mind away. Talk about a good gig! But oh, how the small things please the ignorant. It was very humbling to be in a well-known American investment bank; little me, with access to the doors. It was a timely eye-opener that I might not actually become stiff and robotic if I pursued a career in this industry in the future.

Just after college, I secured my second internship, with a Canadian investment bank. This was the internship that changed my professional life substantially, and this was mainly because I gained a mentor. He was a Canadian fellow who grew up in a small town in Winnipeg, if I remember correctly. He knew what it was like to start working from the bottom and fighting to succeed. He believed in me, a young black female from South East London. I worked my butt off during the internship and made the most of having access to the building, often coming in at 6.30 a.m. to shadow on the trading floor. To this day, I still don't understand the complexities of trading, but at that time, I was just so grateful for the opportunity.

Believe in yourself, receive mercy and find grace—reminds me of Hebrews 4:16

After my second year of university, I secured my third and fourth internships. Yes, two back to back in the same summer. Go me! The first was with another American investment bank and the second was with the same Canadian investment bank. That summer was tough. If I didn't have my faith to sustain me, amongst those varied personalities, I probably wouldn't have survived it. It's easy to forget who the best person is to rely on when you feel like a fish in an ocean, but it was vital that I remembered God as my rock and my comforter.

It was difficult for me to remain confident when in the offices, because naturally all tasks were new. I guess this is where the expression 'fake it until you make it' is applied. I learnt that there really is politics in every organisation; I had just been sheltered from it until that summer. The internships were paid, so I was happy. Thursday nights involved team drinks at the local Slug and Lettuce Bar in Canary Wharf, surrounded by over-enthused peers. It's strange to think that at that time of being so junior, I was oblivious to the existence of any institutional challenges. But rest assured, this awareness came about soon enough. No organisation is perfect, and thankfully, the motion for change has been made.

Be an Entrepreneur

I found it a challenge to secure a graduate job once I left university. I know, shocking, right? With all my internships, I still couldn't seem to ace the final round of interviews. I was discouraged, but I took the opportunity to pursue jobs I wouldn't have typically considered and was so grateful for the time I had to experience them. I'm reminded of the late Aaliyah in her song "Try Again", which encourages listeners to pick themselves up and press on.

Are you ready for the list of roles I gave a go? I worked as a leisure leader, teaching assistant, call centre operative, voluntary charity shop assistant, and even a till operative at a seasonal theme park. This last role was more fun than I had anticipated—who wouldn't be excited about free rides during lunch breaks!

I was finally able to afford much-needed braces—yes, braces!—to boost my confidence and give me that Colgate smile. But unexpectedly, once the braces were removed, my speech remained altered. What can I do, eh? I simply had to accept the things I cannot change and find my confidence in who God says I am rather than society. I say this because of several inappropriate comments made. The orthodontist in West London was one of the most professional I'd ever been to. Well, he still remains the only one I've ever been to, but that doesn't take away from my initial statement.

I took this time to start my self-employed career as a professional CV writer. I'd gained a lot of experience writing CVs for acquaintances whilst at university. I'd attended CV writing days with professional services firms, and had spoken with numerous recruiters about what they'd expect to see in a CV. This two-year adventure was stressful but a lot of fun. I was flattered when my first paid client informed me that she resided in Wales. It took off from there, really. In my opinion, the thing that's worse than the fear of failure is the fear of success. The business was parked, and my focus shifted towards climbing the corporate ladder.

Be a Professional

For nearly two years, I worked with an amazing group of ladies on a project at a FTSE 100 bank. 'Fat Fridays' was an initiative started by a colleague; we'd all get in each other's cars and drive to McDonald's or Burger King for lunch. Although our daily responsibilities were monotonous, and there inevitably were a few team clashes, looking back now, I can honestly say it was by far the least pressured role I've ever been in to date. I moved on after a couple of years to a Japanese bank.

The best thing about working for a Japanese bank was learning about the culture. I could finally eat with chopsticks! Tick on the bucket list. My manager at the time was very strict, but I now see the benefits of that. I needed the push to reach my potential. Of course, one complains while in such a season, but it was a very beneficial experience nonetheless. I learnt to always cover myself, meaning I capture conversations and outcomes in writing, and mind the tone used in emails. I still get friends to proofread 'serious' text messages before sending them.

When we find wisdom, we should keep it tightly in our hands— reminds me of Proverbs 4:6-7

It's important to know oneself, and take necessary actions to accommodate. When you outgrow a role, it's usually time to move on. I took a role as a consultant and had underestimated the demanding nature of the role big time! In this environment, it was important to know what one wanted to be 'famous' for, and then secure projects in that area. Consulting in a large firm isn't easy—all that glitters certainly is not gold.

My first project, for example, involved working two days in Glasgow, two days in Reading and one day in London. Now imagine doing that each week, for months at a time. Yes, I grew in resilience, but also grew closer to burnout. I would advise anyone going into such a role to carry out extensive research before even applying. Flights with British Airways and 4-star hotels aren't the be-all and end-all of life. I'd even discourage anyone from chasing after prestige, but rather to pursue what genuinely makes them happy, what brings satisfaction to the soul. The reality is that money comes and goes, but time is the most precious commodity we have. Value time. Value life.

Be Self-Employed

After many years of professional experience, it made sense to me to become self-employed... again! I love the flexibility and the autonomy since I am my own boss. I strongly recommend that others upskill and take the plunge, especially if life responsibilities are minimal. What's that saying? Nothing ventured, nothing gained. More importantly, commit to the Lord whatever you do, and He will establish your plans (Proverbs 16:3).

CHAPTER 3: IN SICKNESS AND IN HEALTH

"You need to plead with God to do what only He can do, and then you need to get out of the way and let Him do it."

War Room *movie quote*

Be Careful What You Desire

I love to exercise. I love Zumba. Nothing is more thrilling than feeling that burn during a workout. I was more motivated than usual to exercise because I had a holiday booked to Rio de Janeiro, Brazil, at the time of Carnival. I was conscious that I had about three months to tone the bulge found in the central region before the trip. Like most women, I googled Brazil's beaches to get a flavour for how much work I'd have to put into my exercise regime. Was it one of these places I could go to and eat as I pleased? You know, put a few extra pounds on and have nobody notice? Or was it more of a superficial destination with a strong focus on the external appearance? The latter seemed true to me at the time.

Every morning before work, I would throw on my workout clothes, which consisted of baggy trousers and a Lycra crop top. I don't know about anyone else, but I find the more I work out, the more I convince myself it's okay to eat what I want. Oh what a lie! The realisation of this meant that I had to adopt a healthy diet, and quickly. The aim was to consume food full of nutrition but with minimal calories. I decided the most effective way to achieve this was to reduce my intake of carbohydrates, while increasing my fruit and vegetable intake. I also had to become best friends with Mr H_2O, especially to prevent headaches given the temporary diet change. I was committed to working out twice a day, but took rest days. This would be a good time to point out that each workout lasted for up to forty minutes, so technically I wasn't overdoing it. Also, my main evening meals were quite large.

The plan was in full swing and was working better than I expected. At the same time, overtime was on offer at the office. Of course, I jumped at the opportunity to work on the weekends, especially as we would be paid time and a half. What I failed to factor in, however, was the reality that the human body really does need sufficient rest.

No rest for the wicked, rest for the righteous—reminds me of Exodus 33:14

It was a Wednesday evening when I noticed the first abnormality. I began my usual Zumba workout, but found myself panting after just three minutes. I was completely exhausted. I remember my dad walked in, as he usually did, to inform me of how simple and ineffective the routines were. The best advice my dad could give me at the time was to breathe. I had been breathing, so there was no other option but to bail on that workout.

The following day, I walked slowly to my local train station, tapped my Oyster card, proceeded to climb up the stairs and suddenly felt very faint. I quickly found an empty seat on the train platform. A kind lady enquired of my well-being after hearing me gasp ever so deeply for oxygen. I thought I was okay, but obviously I wasn't. My employer was fine with me taking the day off, so I phoned my dad to collect me from the station. It was nice to have a day off from work, although as a contractor it meant I wouldn't get paid. Still, it was only one day off... or so I thought.

The next day I made it into work and my manager gave his diagnostic. After delivering a rather lengthy yet entertaining story about his wife, he concluded that he thought my iron levels might have been low. Clever guy. The blood test results revealed that not only did I have low iron, but I somehow had an unusually operating thyroid. The specialists at the hospital were not remotely comforting when they explained it was an autoimmune condition. Autoimmune? What on earth did that mean? The explanation given was simply that the body attacks itself. When I dug deeper, the specialist informed me that it was possibly triggered by stress. Possibly? My confidence in the healthcare system plummeted instantly. As you can imagine, I was unsatisfied with the specialist's explanation and more impressed with my manager!

Apparently, the hyperthyroidism was not exercise related—the root cause, that is—the specialist's justification that if it was, then all athletes would have it. What I think he failed to consider is that athletes have qualified personal trainers and dieticians advising them. But who knows. The truth is I had, in fact, been working seven days a week, eating healthier, exercising more, and sleeping less.

The Long Road to Recovery

I was on three different medications for my thyroid gland and iron levels, totalling eight tablets a day for ten months and took two and a half months off work. I felt very weak. Everything I ate went right through me—try not to visualise that! My arms became so skinny as my body fed on itself. I remember my mum crying in the kitchen when she saw how skinny I had become. At that time, my uncle was in hospital, dying of cancer, and he also had a stroke, so emotions across the family were high.

The medication was strong. I experienced hair loss and night sweats, as well as aggressive streaks. I believe friends may have seen this once, but family saw it too many times. I even had a fistfight with my younger sister! To be fair, she did provoke me, but irrespective, my behaviour was very out of character and out of order. I even lost my temper on a young man at my birthday dinner for poking my cake. Yes, he was an idiot to do so, but my reaction was very much over the top and the situation was poorly handled. Again, I'd reiterate that the medication was strong. I became skinnier and skinnier each day until the medication finally kicked in and started doing its job. I also became hyper in attitude, despite having little to no energy. Strange combination.

I had a cousin visit and one of my friends. Yes, only one of my friends. They say you know who's there for you when you're at a low. It's so good to visit the sick. That's something I realised while I was a 'victim' to an illness. Good takeaway. The greatest frustration of being unwell was not feeling like my usual self. I felt so dependent on others, which was incredibly uncomfortable at first. Going downstairs for food was too exhausting for me; I needed a more personal service, though I'm not too sure if my siblings appreciated the constant text messages that contained food and drink requests. I must admit, I might've taken advantage once or twice. Or thrice.

Always support others, for one day you will need support— reminds me of 1 Peter 4:9

One afternoon I tried to walk to the local high street. Tried to. I managed to arrive outside of the local shops, but I felt so drained and became emotional due to frustrations with my body.

It's common knowledge that the best way to be successful is to model success. So is the best way to be healed to model someone who was healed? One of my friends at the time told me about Joel Osteen's mother-in-law, who reportedly took a few steps towards her healing from terminal cancer. Steps such as reaching out to people she had offended to make peace with them, as well as living intentionally with each day she had left. It worked for her, and I had no time to waste.

I reached out to everyone I knew who I might've offended over the last few years. It was truly a humbling experience. I had prepared Bible scriptures on the topic of healing to meditate on and daily confessions of these.

As much as I wanted to recover, I also wouldn't have minded not recovering. This world is a mess. I guess I'm one of the few people super excited to get to the other side. I still really want to see my Heavenly Father. But it wasn't in God's plan for me to join Him so soon.

At the same time as I had taken my own steps, my family and friends prayed non-stop and I received my healing. I went for a blood test and they told me my thyroxin hormone levels had stabilised and I no longer needed to take medication. My metabolism was back to normal. Celebration time, right? Well, I couldn't help but think about what I'd now have to forfeit. The new reality I faced was one whereby I could no longer eat pizza, burgers and chocolates without facing the fear of putting on a few extra pounds. However, I was healthy again, which is what mattered. It felt like a fresh chance at life—not that I needed it. Nevertheless, I was going through life with a fresh pair of eyes and an even greater spiritual awareness.

CHAPTER 4: THE HARVEST IS PLENTIFUL, BUT THE WORKERS ARE FEW

"Begin each day like it was on purpose."

Hitch *movie quote*

Selfless Travel

I've travelled often for leisure for the last nine years or so, both with friends and alone. I felt it was time to travel selflessly. Well, let's take it back a step. I had experienced mild depression towards the end of 2016 and had taken a few weeks off from work. I was overworked, like seriously burnt out, and undervalued. There's nothing worse than going into work just for money. There's nothing worse than having a job that's not rewarding. When work becomes your life, and you have no time for anything else, including seeing friends and family, to watch TV or even to read the Bible, that's the time to reassess your current position in life. So on New Year's Eve, I said a prayer to God asking what it is He wanted me to do for Him in the following year. Simply put, I had had enough of being miserable. I felt the Lord drop in my spirit a new direction. I had prayed about it some more and felt complete peace about what He had told me. One of the assignments He had for me was to serve abroad in an orphanage.

Always put into practise what is claimed to be followed— reminds me of James 1:27

Later, the destination of South Africa came to mind. What was even better was that one of my good friends shared the same passion, so she came along too. Two is always better than one. We were both geared up for our first experience of serving abroad. An orphanage in the township of Masiphumelele was the destination. It was located near Cape Town, situated between Kommetjie, Noordhoek and Capri Village. When we first arrived, we were very excited, and we were fine with the accommodation. Oh, how quickly that changed.

It was the long Easter week, which apparently meant the orphanage was closed. Shock horror. How did that make sense? How can an orphanage close? Why did we fly all the way to South Africa? Where did the children stay? So it actually turned out that, despite the project being advertised as an orphanage, it was actually a day care centre. The practise was to keep the orphans within the community to live with relatives and neighbours rather than completely removing them from everything they knew. It was during the daytimes that the younger children attended the orphanage. The older children joined after school.

The owners of the main house were closely linked with the management of the projects that were in operation in the townships. They all had their hearts in the right place, but the owners of the house could be deemed very interesting characters. Pigtails, long skirts and beaded bracelets describes the typical everyday appearance of the middle-aged female owner of the accommodation. The male owner was a hilarious character, bold and slightly socially awkward. In all of my encounters with him, I was never sure if he was fully sober or just unable to have a flowing social conversation. One thing was for sure, it was very empowering to hear of their stories in which they overcame abandonment in their own lives.

I loved serving, the days we were permitted to do so. In the mornings, we were in the nursery. We helped with feedings, played games, and sang songs. There were so many children. The ratio of children to adults must have been twenty to one. The workers, who were elderly women, lived locally, and were referred to as 'Mamas'.

All the children loved having us around. It must've been an added comfort that we looked like them. We listened to them as they read in Klausa, and made them laugh hysterically when we tried to. It was near impossible to form the clicking sound mid-word. I salute anyone who can! We facilitated children's games such as Duck Duck Goose and What's the time, Mr Wolf? We admired them as they played the drums, and we danced with them, enjoying every beat.

It moved our hearts when we were made aware that a number of the orphans had experienced domestic abuse, starvation and rape. It was apparent which children had had it rough. One young boy would eat the leftovers from other children's plates. One young female had been raped three times by her dad when she was younger. When she was younger? She was only thirteen when we met her. I could never imagine what her young existence must've been like, experiencing such fear, violation, anger and heartache.

To be crushed in spirit is a terrible thing—reminds me of Psalm 34:17

Sick in Africa

Serving felt great. Everything was fine, until I started becoming ill. It's strange to think that nights in South Africa could be as cold as what we experienced. The accommodation, bunk-bed style, wasn't the cleanest either, but we were completely fine with it. I caught a cold. I was taking a few medications, but nothing seemed to relieve the symptoms. I shivered at night and felt itchy during the day as the air was dirty.

There were worms and bugs on the floor of the bedroom. I had been given a blanket to stay warm at night—that's when the number of bites tripled! This also happened to two other volunteers. I believe there were about twenty bites on each of my lower legs. I had to change beds. Bed number two seemed fine until the next morning. When my friend came over to visit me, she nearly scared me half to death with her exclamation. She'd noticed that I had been sleeping towards the wall, which had cobwebs with dead flies caught in them. I had to put it out of my mind as a coping mechanism. I changed beds again. Bed number three seemed fine. It was a very good night's sleep. When we returned from volunteering each day, the whole group was often very tired. As I lifted my quilt to get into bed for a nap, I saw a swarm of ants on the top sheet, and under the pillow. There's enduring, and then there's enduring. Discomfort.

The room we were staying in was an annex to the main house. It had a communal sink, and a glass back door, which we were later informed had recently been repaired due to a break-in. While the back door had bolts, it was still made of glass. We slept in fear. In addition to this, the bathroom facilities were outside, and with no outdoor lighting, it became very unsafe to use the facilities after dark. This was the unwritten rule. We experienced discomfort, as you could imagine, as we couldn't relieve ourselves in the evenings. We wouldn't consume food or drink too late.

We could've gone into the main house to use the bathroom facilities, but there were three dogs guarding the doors. As someone who has never been comfortable around dogs, it took me by great surprise that they would charge into our room and push their wet noses between the zips of our luggage. I warmed to them in the presence of others, probably due to social pressure, and played it cool. But if the scenario was ever one on three, them against me, I very much doubt if I'd remain calm.

I was growing tired of not being able to sleep in peace. We all were. I experienced fear of insects, and fear of being burgled. It was hard to rest, even with the aid of the audio Bible or gospel songs which I'd frequently listen to at night.

My symptoms lessened. The dissolvable tablets I had purchased from the local pharmacy were succeeding in making me feel more alive in the mornings, and ceasing the flulike symptoms. But they were causing nosebleeds and aggressive stomach pains. They say no good deed goes unpunished— maybe they're right? I just needed a good night's sleep in a warm environment that was clean.

All Good Things Must Come to an End

When the programme ended, we were prepared to say our goodbyes. It was supposed to be our last night staying there. The plan was to spend a couple of days exploring Cape Town. I couldn't stay that final night, in bed number three. We left that evening and reached civilisation. I still can't bring myself to articulate how comforted I felt when we arrived at the hotel. I saw polished floors, with the absence of bugs. I saw golden banisters and a chandelier in the foyer. I was blown away.

At check-in, I decided to ask the receptionist several vital questions, such as if the bathroom was located inside of the bedroom, or outside of the building, and if the room was carpeted and without bugs. My questions took her by surprise, so much so that she asked if I had been drinking. I had not been drinking. She did confirm, however, and very much to my relief, that bathroom was inside of the hotel room, and the room was bug free.

It was a privilege to arrive in the room, thick quilts, a flat-screen TV on the wall, a clean bathroom and unrestricted hot water. Yes, no more three-minute lukewarm showers. It felt like we'd won the lottery. My friend and I went out to the balcony, and I felt the warm rays from the sun on my cheeks and gave God thanks. We were both so thankful to be free from those living conditions. I felt so guilty to have not been able to tolerate it anymore, but as my health was deteriorating, I had to do what was right for me.

The reality struck me that not everyone can escape such conditions. What was only a few weeks for me was an everyday experience for many people living in those townships. We left South Africa with PTSD. When I arrived at my parents' house, I gave God thanks. When I arrived at my home, I gave God thanks. I would not be ready to undertake such work again in a while, due to the living conditions we were required to endure.

CHAPTER 5: MOVING ON UP

"Money's only something you need in case you don't die tomorrow."

Wall Street *movie quote*

Financial Education

Financial education, or lack thereof, is very prevalent today. I've always been financially disciplined. My dad is a financial disciplinarian—did I just make that term up? There was this one time during secondary school when a Bajan friend invited me to go to the cinema with her. I attended an all-girls' school while she attended a mixed-gender school. Yay, boys!

I asked my dad for permission to go, but there were two conditions that needed to be met first. The first condition was that my older sister would have to go with me. The second condition involved money. My dad gave us three girls (yes, my younger sister too!) thirty-five pounds each. He shared with us what I now believe to be a made-up story about a farmer's boy who had to pay his way to freedom. Then he explained that similarly, if we wanted to go out to the social, we'd have to pay our way to freedom. The fee for freedom was set at seventeen pounds each.

Now believe me when I say that back then, we might as well have been speaking about hundreds of pounds, because it was a lot of money to us. We didn't receive pocket money. Our parents did their best to provide for all our needs. We were taught the value of money left, right and centre. We regularly endured lectures varying from the cost of leaving the light on, to the cost of leaving the fridge door open while deciding which snack to eat. We would stand there for up to two minutes deciding between the banana, apple or pear.

I had to use my only lifeline and phone a friend. I desperately needed advice from my Bajan friend, as I was unsure if I was willing to part ways with the seventeen pounds. It was a no-brainer for her, and she advised us to pay the fee for freedom. We did. I didn't know which movie we were going to see, but the cinema experience, which was infrequent, was fun.

It was a horror movie. I hate horror movies.

Bringing Home the Turkey Bacon

When I landed my first retail job at sixteen, I cherished the £171 I made each month. I told my younger sister the first thing I would do is buy her a pair of shoes of her choice and take her out to the cinema. I honoured this.

We should always ensure that our words align with our actions—reminds me of Matthew 5:37

Working on Sundays meant I couldn't attend church, but fortunately I had Christian ladies on the left and right of me on the tills. There was no straying from the faith. Even in this setting, I remained wise to not purchase food at lunchtimes; I always brought my own sandwiches despite the peer pressure. I was strong-willed. I was born to stand out from the crowd. Go-getters often are.

Solo London Homeowner at 25

I'm a saver. I'm tight. Not because I want to be known as frugal—quite the opposite. I just save for things, acquire them, then save again. Habit. I wanted to move out of my parents' house after university, but renting wasn't an option. It just didn't make financial sense. I saved. I saved hard. I was working for a global firm in an entry-level position, earning eighty pounds a day, and spent ten pounds a week on food. All one really needs is a lunch containing a homemade sandwich, bag of crisps, fruits and perhaps a cheeky chocolate bar.

Every pound in my weekly pay package mattered. I tithed to the local church most of the time, which meant giving away forty pounds of my weekly income. I contributed to the household, paid my phone bill, and had very little of a social life. "If I did go out to eat, I'd eat before I left home and just get a starter from the menu."

When I felt the pressure to save became too much, I'd book a cheap flight to Europe. These flights totalled less than forty pounds for the return journey. Who knew one could enjoy a weekend away for one hundred and fifty pounds, inclusive of food and activities. I'd be lucky to get a decent hotel for that price alone now.

There was one month when I felt so financially constrained that it was like I couldn't breathe. I had to consult my older sister and a good friend, both advising me to loosen up a little ASAP! But how was I meant to loosen up when I had a goal I was determined to reach?

I did loosen up. I had to. I stopped saving for a few months and started spending. It felt so good to not live on a budget. For the last couple of years, it had felt like balancing on a tightrope with alligators waiting beneath to eat me up.

Transitioning back into the mentality of a saver was not easy, but I had to make that transition to reach my savings goal.

Save slowly; slow and steady wins the race—reminds me of Proverbs 13:11

Once I had enough saved for a mortgage deposit, I began the process of house-hunting. The areas I could afford were on the outskirts of London. Every time I made an offer, someone offered more. It became frustrating. I missed family gatherings on weekends because I was committed to house hunting, often scheduling two, three or four back-to-back viewings each weekend. I just couldn't get a break. I gave up.

One of my brothers gave me a pep talk. It was a ten-minute phone call during which he encouraged me to not give up, and that I needed to trust 'the man upstairs' to open the right door. Solo house-hunting really wasn't easy. A couple of days later, one of the agents called me back about a flat which I had previously put an offer in for. The potential buyers had pulled out due to facing financial difficulties; if I wanted the flat, I could have it, as I had made the second-highest offer. I had to think quickly. Pride kicked in, so I politely declined. Not only was the location of the flat far from family and friends, but how dare I be second choice?

That evening, I checked on various websites and saw the market had moved significantly. All properties were priced higher, so much so that I wouldn't even be able to make an offer. So what did I do? I caved. The very next day I rang the agency to see if the flat was still available. It was. Panic over.

While feeling rather smug, I asked if I could reduce my offer, and they unexpectedly said yes. Happy days! Not only had I found somewhere, but I got it cheaper than I had offered. Let's not get carried away though—it was still twenty thousand pounds above the advertised price due to the highly competitive market at the time. It took four months to complete, but the journey was worth it. Every restaurant dinner, bar meetup, and social activity missed was worth it. Me, a young black female who was born into a council flat in Camberwell, South East London, who shared a bed with two other females, and a room with four others in total, had a place of my own. Me, who wore two-pound LidL trainers to school and hand-me-down clothes, had a place of my own.

It was at university when I dreamt of having my own place, and holding faith-based gatherings in it. I had discussed this with a friend who declared and decreed it would come to pass. It was only when I was going through my 'Congratulations on Your First Home' cards when I took time to read the one from my grandparents. I say this because I tend to open cards, take the money out, and close the cards back without reading them. I'm sure many people have this habit whether they'll confess to it or not. The card said "Make this a house of prayer", and right then and there I remembered the conversation I'd had with my friend at university five years prior. Funny that.

Remember to pray not just in religious gatherings—reminds me of Matthew 6:6

Fortunately, when I sent the text out for a prayer meeting, recipients responded. The 'Encouragers' monthly prayer meeting was birthed. It was always going to happen. I mean, I had already been writing encouraging messages over the last few years and circulating these on a weekly basis to people across continents. A message is great for encouragement, but there's something powerful that happens when believers and followers of the Christian faith gather to pray in one accord. A few initiatives have since been birthed and/or watered because of this monthly gathering, and I give God thanks, because it is all for His glory. Obedience to the Father's call really does pay off.

Financial discipline opens doors. I would encourage everyone who sets themselves a financial goal to work hard to achieve it. Create and maintain a spreadsheet for budgeting if necessary. Seek wise counsel to avoid burnout. Surround yourself with destiny helpers and rid yourself of destiny anchors. Always keep your eye on the prize.

CHAPTER 6: THE BIRTH OF FAITH

"Faith is believing something when common sense tells you not to"

Miracle On 34th Street *movie quote*

Birth of Faith

Seventh-Day Adventists assemble to worship on Saturdays. There was a great sense of community within the branch we attended. I recall long skirts and moderately sized hats. At such a young age, I found it impossible to follow the sermon, but I enjoyed this part of the service the most because I was kept entertained. I was fortunate enough to sit on the lap of one of the female teenagers. This young lady taught me how to colour. I mean, she was fully committed to her mission. I wouldn't go as far as to call it a godly assignment, but who knows; this early years training could be the reason why I got an A in art in secondary school. The young lady would take out a sheet of paper from her small handbag, draw several squares, and encourage me to colour them in starting from the top left corner in a diagonal manner. Even though she wasn't family by blood, we were spiritual family; her soul was so gentle.

At age three, I knew she was different, patient, giving, disciplined. It saddened me deeply when I heard that the good Lord had called her home a few years later. She didn't make it to adulthood because the Father wanted her back. This was my first encounter with the death of someone I had actually spoken to in life.

While we were in the Seventh-Day Adventist church, I remember my brothers were in the choir. They sang this chorus so passionately, with actions and stomping as well:

"Marching to Zion Lord, marching hand in hand,
Marching to Zion Lord, marching hand in hand.
It started out, long time ago
Jesus, Jesus, oh how I love you so.
We're marching, we're marching, we're marching to Zion and the Lord."

Pentecostal Church, Here We Come

We left the Seventh-Day Adventist church before I turned five, if I recall. It's important to attend a church which is biblically sound, and at the time, my household felt there were one too many discrepancies between what was practised in the branch and the Bible.

At age seven, I received my first Bible. We had the children's Bible growing up, a gigantic book with a frightening pale guy with a long beard on the front. We'd read this on the Sabbath. I received my very own King James Version Bible from my grandma's Pentecostal church. There was genuine excitement because I loved the stories. My grandparents took us to their church—my sisters and me, that is. I enjoyed Sunday school, although at that age, I was already aware of biblical discrepancies due to homeschooling, discrepancies between what was being taught and my own understanding. What I loved about this church was the strong family feel. Come to think of it, that could've been because the majority of our families were related.

I loved the annual summer convention. It was a chance to see cousins and friends from different branches, but also a chance to dress up. We laid out our clothes each night for the next morning. My sisters, one of the cousins and I would even plan to coordinate our outfits. We had a Youth Day annually, in which branches of the church would compete against each other. My favourite activity was 'Bible drill', which involved reciting the sixty-six books of the Bible in chronological order.

The joys of church games—reminds me of Psalm 4:7

At age fourteen, I gave my life to Christ for the third—or was it fourth?—time during one of the annual summer church conventions. I can't believe that when young hearts were opened to the Lord at the altar, and when the sinners' prayer was prayed, those young souls were declared to be saved, but without receiving any explanation as to what that actually meant; there were zero follow-ups. Such was my experience, and many others' too in that congregation at that time. This was a place where, despite good intentions of the older generation, there was insufficient accountability to the younger generation at that time. Let's put it this way: the first place I was ever offered weed was in that church branch. The first place I ever saw a condom was in that church branch. Had the older generation known what was going on at that time, they certainly would have put a stop to it. Let's leave it at that. It soon became apparent to me that, if I was going to try out this 'Christianity', I would have to do so outside of that church branch. But we'll come to that shortly.

That same summer, at age fourteen, a gentle soul, a female who attended another branch of that church, prayed with me that I would receive a supernatural understanding of God. She was spirit filled, a pastor's daughter. My life was never the same again after that moment.

"Real real real, Christ so real to me
I love him, 'cause he gave us the victory

Many people doubt him
But I can't live without him,
That is why I love him so, he's so real to me."

One of the songs I loved from that church. It spoke volumes to me then, and still does now. I left that church. As I said, that one prayer changed my life. That prayer! I desired to know the Lord for myself, so I began reading the scriptures with a hunger I had never experienced before. Rather than reading a boring book, which had been my previous perception and experience, this book called the Bible now contained stories of love and romance, war and jealousy, poems and mysteries. I couldn't put it down!

Eyes Wide Open

I was taken on a journey of spiritual growth that led me away from this church. It was the protection of God. On my journey, I witnessed the supernatural gifts of the spirit. The first church I went to outside of my family church was located near Elephant and Castle in South East London; it was a Nigerian church and was full of disciplined youth. It was refreshing to see.

I was amazed when the Sunday school was segregated by gender across two rooms. At the time, I was unsure if this was a good or a bad thing. Should kids at that age be made aware of gender differences? Should they be allowed to learn together? I was in no position to formulate an opinion based on their practises, so I simply observed and wondered. "Eh eh eh eh, my God is good ohh"—a song that was sung weekly. It will forever cause me to stand up and struggle to simply two-step in a sophisticated manner, because the drums alone in this song entice one to dance properly. This church was not to be my home. There was more of the body of Christ to see, experience and fellowship with.

Unexpectedly, I was invited by a college friend to visit another Nigerian church but in East London, which had a well-established Thursday night youth ministry. There are current gospel artists who came out of that ministry; they did very well to educate and normalise obedience to Christ within social circles that were possibly mainly secular. It was suddenly cool to stand for the things of God. What an amazing community to be a part of at that age. This church was not to be my home.

The next church I was led to visit seemed to be gifted in casting out demons from people, something I had never been exposed to and had never truly believed still happened in modern-day society. That was until I witnessed it first-hand with a few other teenagers I knew locally. It was difficult to not believe in what was happening right in front of my eyes. I remember hearing the lead pastor boldly declare, "May the chief spirit within this child of God manifest itself right now", and this was always followed by a manifestation. The spirit would then be banished to Hell, and the person would be free, as demonstrated by an awakening out of a trance-like state with no recollection of what had happened before. Scary stuff! This church was not to be my home.

The next church I was called to not only visit but be a part of for the next few years was during university, where I decided to be baptised and live wholeheartedly to honour the Lord. I'm not sure why it took so long; I was eighteen, but at least by this age, I was fully aware of what I was forfeiting. With this decision came life restrictions, but life freedoms too. The church in Brighton created a fantastic platform in which I was able to learn the morals of the faith, and enjoy worship and an intimacy with God unknown to many believers I knew at the time. I have come across many who are afraid to be impacted emotionally by the Lord, but when we do let go completely, it's such a refreshing experience. To be baptised in the Holy Spirit is quite the experience, if you so choose to believe in the possibility of this as stipulated in the Bible—turn to John and Corinthians.

This seems like a good time to tackle the contentious topic of 'tongues'. Do I speak in tongues? No. Did I speak in tongues? The elders said I did. Is speaking in a tongue my gifting? I would say not. Do I believe in tongues? Yes, although we might disagree on the sound. Do I believe I lack because I do not speak in tongues as a gift? No. Am I gifted in other ways? Yes, many. Glad we cleared that up. Does anyone else occasionally have a conversation with themselves? Yes, we are all sane.

The joys of indescribable peace—reminds me of Psalm 29:11

After university, I found it very difficult to find a sound church. I had a heart to serve, so I went to a large congregation where I served on three teams. There was such a strong emphasis on serving in the house, so much so that being spiritually fed on a Sunday took a back seat and in fact became something I longed for. I had to continuously self-feed, and by this I mean read the Bible independently and watch sermons online. How can a shepherd allow its flock to work all day on an empty stomach?

One Sunday, I was watching channel TBN and heard a powerful yet amusing sermon from a Caribbean pastor. I had to check out the church. It would appear it was where the Lord wanted to plant me, for the time being anyway. I give God thanks that there's a strong emphasis in knowing the Bible. Honestly, my desire to grow the number of believers in God and the number of followers of Jesus's teachings was a fire reignited, and is fanned on a weekly basis.

And the journey continues.

Spiritual Behaviours

I've had... let's call it the 'privilege', for now, of being exposed to many different Christians and many different personalities over the last decade. It seems increasingly common for many to adopt a stance of perceived 'holiness', as if it could ever look just one way. I was 100 percent guilty of this. It's like on top of living a clean lifestyle, there's a need to look holy and sanctified. Why was I like this? Why do so many do this?

Let's dig deeper.

I'm guilty of being so concerned with what others thought of me, when all that mattered and continues to matter is what God thinks of me. He sets the standard, not others. Not people, and certainly not established cultural norms. I had to accept that I didn't need to seek external validation, period. So what exactly did I used to do? Hold back the laughter, if you can.

I'd sound holy. Let sounding holy fool no man, for it is God who sees the heart. Has anyone else changed the way they speak when in godly settings? For example, when in church, I'd throw in a few "amens" in conversation rather than "yes, I agree with you", but outside of church, "amen" would never leave my mouth, if not for at the end of a prayer. I suppose it's like when teenagers speak in what can be described as a 'hood' or 'street-like manner' when with friends, then speak completely differently when with their parents. Within the Christian faith, is there a need to have varied voices as described? Food for thought.

I'd look holy. Let looking holy fool no man, for it is God who sees the heart. I'd change the way I appeared to others by being slightly more serious than usual. It was my face. Am I the only one who's ever put on that straight, intense face especially after praying? Why do we do this? There's no one way to look after praying to God. I suppose my thoughts at the time were if I tightened up my face and looked angry, those around me would believe I was praying and petitioning with passion. Now I tend to smile after praying. This tends to throw people off, but I'm smiling with the certainty that God will take over and I don't need to stress. How can I frown when I believe that?

I'd be quiet. Let a quiet disposition fool no man, for it is God who sees the heart. When in a new setting, it's common to quieten down. But when one susses out the group or congregation, it's common to become slightly louder. But continuing to take on a quiet persona to appear to be gentler than one is swerves to self and people-pleasing, desiring human acceptance, and deceiving self and others. We become like a child who's careful to say anything not out of wisdom but to fit in to this unusual culture of being a certain way.

I'd be loud and eloquent. Let eloquence fool no man, for it is God who sees the heart. I've been in church settings where what was respected was being vocal. In some church groups, the focus was on being vocal about life experiences. I recall a small group session where I had to clutch at straws to contribute a relevant life experience. In others, the focus was on knowing Bible scriptures—or should I say appearing to know Bible scriptures—to contribute. The pressure was on in this instance. Now it might sound good, but in reality it swerved to self once again, because my heart didn't want to spend those thirty minutes preparing to encourage others but rather to look knowledgeable in front of others. We were all caught up.

Authenticity is vital—reminds me of Romans 12:9

This chameleon behaviour needed to stop. I had to decide to be myself in every setting. Take me or leave me. God loved me for me. He disliked this behaviour because this wasn't me adapting my behaviour depending on the company I was around and so being all things to all men to benefit the Kingdom, as described in 1 Corinthians 9:19-23, but rather this was me being all things to all men to benefit myself socially. I was not born to fit in. It's worth repeating: I was not born to fit in.

This inherited church culture, particularly amongst the ethnic community in my experience, had me and those around me programmed to continue to look the part. Now, most of us were the part anyway, but learning to 'play' the church by mimicking behavioural traits that had people-pleasing at the heart was not the path God wanted me to stay on.

It took a few years for me to realise that God isn't after any of this! He loves me just the way I am, and so much so that He won't leave me as I am. He designed me, all of me, my personality and my quirks. If others didn't like it, that was not and remains not my concern. For example, I tend to be direct in speech, and while I can be diplomatic when required, this isn't my natural stance. To reject who I am and how I am is to reject our great God's unique creation. We can't all be the same, nor should we try to be.

Spiritual Recruitment

We all have slightly different interpretations of how we should live out the Christian recruitment lifestyle. I've been around many who believe Christians should pull away from non-believers and focus on the community of believers, but in the same breath expect these same Christians to invite friends, relatives and colleagues to church. Did you catch the contradiction? The thing is, I've been that person. I've encouraged Christians who were new to the faith to pull away from all supposed negative influences because we know bad company corrupts good character. Then I've encouraged more mature Christians—this is a judgement in itself, which I am unqualified to make—to stay in non-Christian circles and be a light in a dark place in terms of being an example of Jesus to non-believers. Now, as you can tell, one can't both run from the dark and let their light shine in the dark at the same time.

I don't believe Christians should do any running unless chasing after the Lord. I play the long game. It's the only way I've personally experienced genuine conversion. Genuine fruitful conversion. By this, I mean a person decides to follow the teachings of Jesus Christ rather than just being 'spiritual'.

CHAPTER 7: ENCOURAGEMENTS

"Where we're going, we don't need roads."

Back to the Future *movie quote*

Bring Down Those Walls

When Joshua fought the battle of Jericho, the walls came tumbling down. If the walls of Jericho represent the religious façade adopted by myself or others, then I'm about to pull the walls of Jericho down, at least for myself. I hope you'll join me!

The Lord challenged me to be a living testimony of His goodness, recording the good, the bad and the ugly areas of my life for His glory. I believe when I hide areas I struggle with, I rob God of His glory because He restores me, I do not restore me. The Bible scripture in Psalm 84:11 indicates that those in Christ, whose walk is blameless, will lack no good thing. Therefore, I will continue to embrace justification and take courage that the process of sanctification is taking place every day. I am confident that my present shortcomings will be made whole in time.

I am purposed to be an encourager, to uplift the downhearted, to re-convince every person who believes they've failed beyond recovery that they're wrong. We all face daily struggles, but we stand from a point of victory! God is not dead. Jesus lives!

I am purposed, at least for now, to serve others by encouraging them with life experiences and with Bible scriptures. I am purposed to write down the daily revelations I see, to encourage others not to be overwhelmed with their shortcomings. By faith, I have the mind of Christ and live for the Lord's approval, no one else's.

I pray that this final section encourages you, and that you realise you're not alone in your process of sanctification. The Lord will pursue you endlessly during this journey on earth. Enjoy the ride!

SERVANTHOOD

Servanthood Doesn't Switch Off

When we're saved, we're called to mission. This becomes a constant way of life; it doesn't switch off.

I've noticed that whenever I need to climb stairs with a heavy suitcase at the station, unexpectedly there is always someone at that precise moment to help, usually a guy. Let's call that provision from above. The other day, I witnessed this for someone else as I journeyed to volunteering at a homeless drop-in over a weekend. A lady with a buggy was helped up the first flight of stairs... but the man ran off after. As she approached the second and final flight of stairs, I was looking around for a guy to help her but there was no one. There was only me. So I helped her.

What did the Lord challenge me on?

(1) Sometimes it's us who He has called to use in service of others

Are we ready to be used to help another, for the Lord's glory? Or are we spectators waiting for the Lord to use somebody else? Are we saying, "Lord, send me!" in line with Isaiah 6:8?

(2) Be prepared to be called to serve at any time

Do we need to shift our perspective to accept that servanthood can be an inconvenience? Are we ready to be used only when we choose to be ready? Servanthood is not like a light switch. It does not switch on and off—it stays on!

The Bible scripture in Matthew 9:37 (NIV) says: "Then He [Jesus] said to His disciples, 'The harvest is plentiful, but the workers are few.'" It's good to keep this in mind every day.

I would be guilty of deceiving you if I didn't reveal that part of me during the experience outlined above asked God, "Why me?" But what nonsense is that? Either I want to be used for the Lord's glory or I don't.

Are we going to contribute to the group of workers? While it's great to have things work out in our favour, we're often the instruments in granting favour to others. Let's try to always have a willing nature.

Be encouraged to be a full-time server of the Lord.

Dinner for Two

It seems quite common to hear Christians express a lack of interest in being around non-Christians. However, there is such beauty and power in connecting with non-Christians, and sowing seeds of light.

I'm reminded of Mark 2:16 (NIV), which says: "When the teachers of the law who were Pharisees saw him eating with the sinners and tax collectors, they asked his disciples: 'Why does he eat with tax collectors and sinners?'"

Way back then, there was a "holier than thou" mindset, to not be in the company of 'sinners' socially. This mindset remains today in many Christians; it's as if the perception is that they can catch sin.

I propose we consider the following five points below:

(1) Don't be a Pharisee

Jesus dined with sinners (Mark 2:16). We were all sinners (Romans 3:23), saved by grace though faith (Ephesians 2:8-9). I'm sure we still sin from time to time in action, or even in thought (1 John 1:8). We are no better than anyone else. We do not have it all figured out. We are perfectly in process. Let's not look down on people.

(2) Be around them

Some Christians remove all non-believers from their lives, from their social circles. This cannot be right. We're called to be a light in a dark place (John 1:5). How can we be a light in a dark place if everyone around us is beaming with light? We should not fear that the darkness will corrupt the light, but have confidence in the Lord that the light in us will break through the darkness.

(3) Remember who you once were

We are born again now (John 3:1-21), but we weren't always. We too used to indulge in the world, and even if the Lord was 'always' with us, we may not have been fully committed to Him. We are to treat people how we would like to be treated (Matthew 7:12), with love. Let's not turn our nose up at people who have different struggles to us, or a struggle we overcame a while back. Humility and understanding are key.

(4) Control your passion

It's very off-putting when people Bible bash. Often it comes from a good place—a strong inner desire to see transformation—but this method is truly ineffective. A recent article from *Premier* referred to this method as 'spiritual abuse'. The reality is we can't save people, only God can! Yes, He can use us as instruments in His plan, but we must play our part in obedience, then let go. We are to sow seeds of light and let it grow rather than expect a tree to grow overnight. And when we don't see that tree, we shouldn't dig around in the soil and somehow try to force a seed to grow.

(5) Be an example

It's a real shame when believers forget their journey, I mean what they've been saved from. By associating with non-believers, we're able to be an example of Jesus to those living how we used to live, to those who think how we used to think. Sometimes we're the only Jesus they see, which reminds me of the powerful song called "The Last Jesus," by Kirk Franklin. Believe it or not, non-believers do notice when we go quiet during certain conversations. They notice when we decline to attend certain social events. It often causes reflection on what's being discussed, and it even reflects on the nature of the events. This is what we want! We want to spark awareness of a different way of being.

Be encouraged to be the salt of the earth and the light of the world (Matthew 5:13-16).

Same Old Same Old

Have you ever experienced déjà vu when reading the Bible scriptures? Situations often repeat themselves. Ecclesiastes 1:9 (NIV) says: "What has been will be again, what has been done will be done again; there is nothing new under the sun." The reality of this has smacked me in the face through the scriptures on many occasions, but I will highlight two for you.

Lesson 1: Situations repeat

While listening to the audio Bible—at night, which heightened my emotional response in the moment—I stumbled across Judges 19:22-25, which has strong similarities to Genesis 19:5-8. Because of the horrid nature of the text, I will not go into detail, but in each story, individuals pursued perverse desires against the will of others. Not the best story to potentially fall asleep to, but nonetheless a good reminder that wickedness carried out back then remains today.

Lesson 2: Behaviours repeat

In Genesis 3:10, we see Adam confessing that he tried to hide his physical self from the almighty, all-knowing God. Later, in Genesis 18:15, we see Sarah tried to hide the truth that she laughed at what the Lord had said would happen. Both instances make me chuckle, as it's as if both characters forgot who God is, that He's omniscient. While Adam confessed, Sarah failed to do so, but both tried to hide.

Both lessons 1 and 2 are good reminders that we shouldn't be caught off guard. Let's not be surprised when situations arise again, or when we experience unpleasant behavioural traits in people again. The obstacles we face may very well pop up again in time. The characters in our personal stories may change, but ultimately we come up against the same spirits repeatedly, and the same behaviours, be it to provoke us, to deceive us, to break our confidence, etc. Being a servant of the Lord is not easy in this world, but we can take comfort in knowing that there is no element of surprise; rather we should pre-empt situations and behaviours with discernment.

Moving forward:

(1) Let's continue to maintain our effective prayer lives, laying our petitions at the Lord's feet, as self-reliance leads to nowhere fast. The Holy Spirit brings to our remembrance scriptures for declaration, relevant Bible stories to encourage us at the right time, past situations we have faced and overcome, and uplifting songs.

(2) Let's consider keeping a log of experiences so we don't forget what we've been through, and what we've overcome. By doing so, when it—whatever it is—returns, we can recall that we already dealt with and overcame it.

(3) Let's engage with our support network, checking in periodically, as they can be great reminders of past challenges and victories provided they are kept in the loop during our journeys.

Be encouraged to remain on guard each day, to not easily forget what has already been faced, and to stand firm as an overcomer.

Be Humble, Sit Down

I had a dream in which I was at a dinner, and there was complete silence. In the dream, one of my long-term friends who sat across the table from me broke the silence by exclaiming, "Be humble!" The comment came from nowhere and took me by surprise.

When I woke up, I was in a foul mood. I had been offended by the dream and didn't agree with what had been said. Throughout the day, this same dream circled my mind until I reached a point of agreeing that God knows me better than I know myself. At that point I chose to openly receive the explanation from the dream. We may think we know ourselves, but we have blind spots. God always knows us best.

God challenges us through different channels, and on areas we may think we've mastered. Now God may want to point out to us that we have character flaws. We might have a foul tongue, or be selfish, envious, spiteful, deceitful, lack self-control or something else—of course, not all at the same time! But you know what, it's okay! Because when we're in a relationship with the Lord, He cleans us up as we journey through life. That's right, we aren't doomed to remain the same, but can and will be better.

Servanthood is usually thought of as performing duties for the Lord, but I'd like to think of it from another perspective here, of being subject to the direction of another. 2 Corinthians 12:9 (NIV) says: "For my [God's] power is made perfect in [our] weakness", which means a weakness in our character is an opportunity for God to show up, show off, and help us to change to resemble Jesus. When we are subject to God, we should never feel condemned for a weakness but rather continue to pray about them. Perhaps the Lord has exclaimed to you to be patient, forgiving or to have self-control.

Be encouraged to accept God's correction and be obedient; He knows us better than we know ourselves.

Faulty Doctor's Note

How many times have we found ourselves mentioning an area we're working on in our personal lives, or a situation we're facing, and someone enthusiastically offers a lot of advice but without having fully understood what the issue or situation was, the history, the cause, or the progress to date?

As servants of the Lord, we can be overzealous to support those around us, but James 1:19 tells us to be slow to speak and quick to listen. I'm reminded of Acts 16:16, where the female slave is so overzealous for declaring who Paul and his companion were that Paul became annoyed and commanded the spirit to come out of her in the name of Jesus Christ. Let's mind our zeal, ensuring the origin is the Holy Spirit and nothing else.

Not only should we be quick to listen to hear the full situation someone is going through, but we're instructed by Ecclesiastes 12:13 to always aim to hear the end of the matter before forming a conclusion. My question is how do we stop the urge to offer our 'expert guidance' prematurely?

Advice 1: Address motives

Are we keen on supporting the person, or keen on having our say? If we're keen to have our say or be heard, why is this? I pray we all grow in humility.

Advice 2: Address characteristics

Are we displaying patience when we cut people off in conversation to contribute our thoughts? How must it make the other person feel? Are we rushing others because we don't have sufficient time to hear the end of the matter? If so, how can we write a prescription? I pray we all grow in patience.

Advice 3: Care for others

Are we genuinely caring about the person if we're not investing the time to hear the full story? Are we caring for them if we aren't giving them a chance to elaborate on what they're sharing for us to have a better understanding? We won't be able to share the most relevant experiences from our lives to support others if we don't take time to genuinely care for them.

Be encouraged to be better in your communication with others.

Time of Reflection

As servants of the Lord, we might occasionally feel a sense of regret because we run on God's timing rather than our own. Due to impatience, we might find ourselves unsettled about waiting on something from God which we could technically get for ourselves outside of His will. Perhaps there is something, or someone even, that we really desire to have but are still yet to receive it. On this matter, I have some great news for us all! God is not bound by time. He's outside of time and knows exactly when it's best to grant us our heart's desires, per His will.

Jeremiah 32:17 (NIV) says: "Ah, Lord God! Behold, You have made the heavens and the earth by Your great power and outstretched arm. There is nothing too hard for You." There is certainly nothing too hard for God.

Let's continue to have hearts full of gratitude and remember what God has already done. Over the years, I've personally witnessed marriages and engagements, businesses have started, people have qualified in their respective professional fields, people have cleared debts on credit cards and student loans, many have lost weight and a few who wanted to have gained weight, some have worked abroad, gained investments, or completed mission trips for the Kingdom. Sometimes we just need to take a step back and believe that God is God. He has kept us through many seasons, and while I'm sure we all continue to face many trials and tribulations, we're still standing!

Be encouraged to hold on to the memories of what God has done in the past, to have confidence in what He can do in the future.

Home Truths

As one family in Christ, we may attend different congregations, but we remain one body. Let's first review a few relevant scriptures.

1 Corinthians 12:13 (NIV) says: "For we were all baptized by one Spirit so as to form one body—whether Jews or Gentiles, slave or free—and we were all given the one Spirit to drink."

Ephesians 4:4-5 (NIV) says: "There is one body and one Spirit, just as you were called to one hope when you were called; one Lord, one faith, one baptism."

Acts 10:34-35 (NIV) says: "Then Peter began to speak: 'I now realize how true it is that God does not show favouritism but accepts from every nation the one who fears Him and does what is right.'"

I love these scriptures, especially Peter in the book of Acts, who realises after a vision from the Lord and real-life experiences that God could also save the Gentiles. I love how inclusive our God is. There is not one broken vessel He can't mend, not one stone He leaves unturned.

Being one family, we share a common life purpose, which some religious institutions have distorted over the years. It was only after I attended an event in which false doctrine was communicated to many that my spirit felt stirred to explicitly shut down the lies of the enemy regarding our life purposes. When seeking out a church, please ensure the doctrine is sound. When transitioning between congregations, let's really listen to the Holy Spirit before we move. Time for some home truths, as I call them.

Home Truth 1: Obedience

We live to glorify our Lord and Saviour Jesus Christ who walked on earth, shed His blood for us on the cross of Calvary, and rose again defeating death, and by doing so bridged the gap between humanity and God. We have a unified purpose to live to be obedient to our Lord. We do not live to benefit ourselves. We do not live for fame or fortune. We do not live for our bank balance to grow. We live to please our Heavenly Father, as encouraged in 1 Thessalonians 4:1. If God tells us to sell our possessions, or to leave our high-profile jobs, or even people, we should be obedient. Let's never allow any earthly thing to take hold of our hearts but always be willing to give it up. The reality is that we're just passing through earth, so let's not become too attached to anything, or anyone.

Home Truth 2: Winning souls

Evangelism is so central to our individual and collective Christian walk. Mark 16:15 commands us to proclaim the gospel to the whole of creation. I think we'd all agree that it's the best thing ever when someone chooses to make Jesus reign over their lives. Luke 15:10 tells us that there is rejoicing in the presence of the angels of God when one sinner repents. We do not aim to win souls to 'a' church; we aim to win souls to 'the' church, which is to the body of Christ. Life is not about business, assets, status, or pleasing others. These things cannot be our idols. They are not God.

Home Truth 3: Jesus at the centre

We do not enter the presence of God to make a church famous on social media, or to be a part of a 'movement'. Jesus should always remain as the focal point of our lives. Let's assess our hearts regularly, as some desires may not align to God's will. Trust me, I had to give up the desire to live in Spain, which was deep-rooted, but it wasn't aligned to the will of God for my life. Let's keep Jesus at the centre of our hearts, and our churches. Let's always continue to pray for our leaders. May the Holy Spirit continue to lead us all into truth and protect us from being caught up in anything that doesn't glorify our Lord and Saviour.

Be encouraged to read the Bible and keep Jesus at the centre of life.

BATTLEFIELD

Every Coin Has Two Sides

It was a Tuesday afternoon, and it began to pour down with rain. I saw many people getting soaked, but there I was feeling happy I had packed my umbrella that day. I was walking back to the office after lunch when I noticed a pedestrian but kept walking. As I was walking, I felt God tell me to walk back and give my umbrella to the pedestrian. I chose not to—it was wet! As a black lady with natural hair, I can assure you I didn't want the acidic rain touching my roots! I'm personally not a frizzy hair fanatic; however, this became a secondary concern.

I considered walking, but as I began to feel physical discomfort, I knew I had to be obedient. So I walked back to find the pedestrian still standing there waiting to cross the road. He was a blind man with a stick. He must've been waiting to hear the beeps. I dashed towards him and offered my umbrella; he expressed gratitude but politely declined. Strange, I thought. Was this some sort of test? I believe it was.

God does test our obedience from time to time. He checks if we know His voice, and I reckon He probably even tracks how quick we are to respond. I've come to realise that following the Christian faith isn't always a walk in the park. Yes, that's right, it's not always rosy. We're supposed to follow him come rain or shine, which is an interesting expression, as it captures the reality that there are rainy seasons. Sometimes it feels like we're on a battlefield, battling between choosing our Father's will or choosing our own. Especially when you're an independent person or tend to be self-reliant, relying in God and following His lead does not always come naturally. We should be dedicated to God whether the coin flips and lands on heads or tails. I guess the perspective to keep is that God knows what He's doing, and it's always us who need to get in line.

2 John 1:6 (NIV) says "And this is love; that we walk in obedience to his commands. As you have heard from the beginning, his command is that you walk in love."

We should be committed to walking in obedience and love. The reality is that God sustains us even if we do give something away, so rather than battling God and losing, it's better to be on the winning side. This reminds me of an old Caribbean chorus which says, "Jesus is the winner man".

I believe Anthony Evans says it best in his rendition of "Blessed Be Your Name", where we're reminded that the name of the Lord should be reverenced whether we're in the land that's plentiful or the road marked with suffering. Now handing over my brolly isn't at all considered suffering, but I'm aware that some are led to hand over much more, which could seem like suffering.

Be encouraged to hold on to the faith during the seasons of rain, continuing to walk in obedience, growing closer to the Lord through the season.

Paranoia. Silence it.

I don't know about you, but there's nothing that freaks me out more than walking on the pavement and hearing footsteps behind me! Usually I wait a while to see if the person will take a different route, but when it's persistent, I tend to cross over the road. My mind creates a new reality where there is a seven-foot strong geezer behind me waiting to attack. It's foolish really, especially as 2 Timothy 1:7 (KJV) says "For God hath not given us the spirit of fear..." The mind can be a battlefield. Well, my mind can be, anyway.

But I was shown something recently. As I was walking home in the land of greenery—Bexley residents rock!—I was the person tailgating another. The lady was blonde, middle-aged, tall and confident. She didn't pause at any point to pretend to do that usual handbag check for keys or phone. She didn't even turn around to get a glimpse of what I looked like; she just confidently continued her path.

How was it that she had such peace? Was she a Christian? Wasn't I supposed to be walking fearless in peace? You know, walking with a comprehendible peace, an unshakeable calm. The scenario prompted me to question and to reflect on the depths of my belief. I'm sure we all could deepen our everyday faith, to honestly grasp the reality that the Lord walks with us, and protects us.

Surely the scenario doesn't stop with me, or you, thinking someone dangerous could be walking behind us. What about that paranoia that someone is out to get us, in our family, in our friend circle, at work, or at church even? I pray we'll have true peace in abundance in every aspect of our lives. And when we feel we don't, I pray we'll recognise this in our thoughts and silence it! I pray we'll speak out the Bible scriptures, declaring truth. Instructions are given in John 14:1, and John 14:27 (NIV) reiterates this: "...Do not let your hearts be troubled and do not be afraid." These are the scriptures I now consciously declare when I feel shaken.

Philippians 4:7 (NIV) says: "And the peace of God, which transcends all understanding, will guard your hearts and our minds in Christ Jesus." Do I believe this? Do you believe this? Let's choose to believe this!

Be encouraged that although we're all a work in progress, as we become more self-aware, we'll improve and get 'there' in the end, wherever there is.

In Recovery

Sometimes I'm happy, really happy. Sometimes I'm sad, really sad. I believe David experienced something similar in the Book of Psalm.

Psalm 42:5 (NIV) says: "Why, my soul, are you downcast? Why so disturbed within me? Put your hope in God, for I will yet praise him, my Saviour and my God."

Psalm 42:11 (NIV) says: "Why, my soul, are you downcast? Why so disturbed within me? Put your hope in God, for I will yet praise him, my Saviour and my God."

Psalm 43:5 (NIV) says "Why, my soul, are you downcast? Why so disturbed within me? Put your hope in God, for I will yet praise him, my Saviour and my God."

No, your eyes are not playing tricks on you! I did just write out the same verse three times! Why? Because David repeated himself three times. 'Downcast' and 'disturbed' were the words David used. The common interpretation is that David was depressed. Fair enough, as it seems increasingly common these days to have experienced a level of depression at some point. But I wonder if we've experienced this feeling of disturbance in our souls before. Have we ever experienced a real troubling at our core? I've only experienced it once due to cult exposure— don't ask!—but it took a lot to lift the feeling, including prayer and fasting.

So what causes such a disturbance? A deep disturbance at our core can be caused by a realisation of a truth that opposes our initial understanding or core belief. For example, if during our teenage years, we were informed that we were adopted, or if we receive healing and then the illness returns, or if we see brothers and sisters who we regarded as spiritual mentors fall by the wayside. The cause of the disturbance could be an unexpected struggle to conceive, or even experiencing first-hand for the first time that the 'system' might be rigged against a certain demographic of people.

But how does the Bible speak to such deep discomfort, disappointment, and hurt? Well, David advised us to "put our hope in God", which is to desire and expect resolution from God. David said, "...for I will yet praise Him", which is to adore God irrespective of what we face. David also said, "...my Saviour and my God", which is demonstrating perspective of who God is and what He did for us.

Recovery from a low is possible. Everyone has lows. Some people's lows last longer than others'. It's easy to categorise feelings as depression in a world that says we need to be happy all the time. Experiencing a level of sadness is normal (John 11:35). While it might not bring us comfort that David repeated himself, it reveals the human need to keep at it until the grey cloud has lifted. The mind can be a battlefield.

Be encouraged that grey clouds do pass with time, so keep praying, and keep activating the power within.

He Disciplines Daily

Since becoming more conscious of the spirit within, I've noticed daily discipline. It's great to have accountability—but if your accountability partners fall off track, and if your pastor or pastoral care team in church are rarely accessible, then you find yourself solely reliant that the Holy Spirit will keep you in check.

Psalm 121:3-4 (NIV) says: "He will not let your foot slip—he who watches over you will not slumber; indeed, he who watches over Israel will neither slumber nor sleep." I'm so grateful our God will not let our feet slip. He would rather discipline us daily than leave us to our own devices.

When we pray for our thoughts to be obedient to Christ (2 Corinthians 10:5), the Lord really does come through. The mind can be a battlefield, so how does the Holy Spirit discipline our thoughts daily? This is different for each of us, and I've heard of a variety of methods, the most common being bringing scriptures to the forefront of the mind. Here's a bit of humour for you, but it's very true: during one season, whenever I'd have a negative thought, my right foot would stub the ground mid-thought!

For example, when I'd be around people on public transport and witness them behaving rather idiotically—toned that down three times—certain thoughts would come to mind along the lines of *The Purge*. Seen that movie? So mid-thought, I'd take a step due to being shoved and my right foot would stub the ground. When it first started happening, I thought I was experiencing a breakdown in my nervous system. But then after seeking answers from our Father, the cause was revealed, and it was my inappropriate thoughts at the time. To go a step further, I'd confess that the thoughts were often dwelled on, rather than dismissed.

Another example is one night, as I walked home from the local train station, I couldn't help but thinking of one of my colleagues choking on crisps. I let the thought play through, and chuckled extensively, in fact. That day my colleague was truly awful, and although I maintained professional composure and was prayerful to keep my peace, it must be true that part of me liked to entertain that thought.

Jeremiah 4:14 (NIV) says: "Jerusalem, wash the evil from your heart and be saved. How long will you harbor wicked thoughts?" This scripture is very powerful and spoke directly to my situation. That night, I had to repent and pray for myself as well as for my colleague. I felt like Isaiah 6:5 was describing me, a ruined person.

Such things are not a rarity, and I say this to be completely transparent at the risk of human judgement, because we live for the approval of God, not man (Galatians 1:10). I pray there is no visibility of correction in the physical for anyone else, as it was being an embarrassing season!

Be encouraged to be open to discipline and learn from it quickly. Be encouraged to let God into the ugliest parts of us (1 John 1:8) for Him to work.

As Small as a Mustard Seed

My sisters know how much I enjoy watching both movies and TV series that contain a supernatural element. I'm a huge fan of programmes such as *Joan of Arcadia* and *Medium*. Can you guess the gift?

One of my sisters recommended I watch *Little Boy* (2015), and boy, did it move my heart. Why, you may ask? Well the main character did not have any supernatural powers, but he did have faith. Because in its purest form, the movie touched on three important lessons that I believe are relevant to each of us today. The lessons relate to faith, and I'm reminded of Matthew 17:20 (NIV), which says: "...Truly I tell you, if you have faith as small as a mustard seed, you can say to this mountain, 'Move from here to there,' and it will move. Nothing will be impossible for you."

Let's look at the lessons.

Lesson 1: Our Father is on the battlefield

The boy tried to use powers, which he was convinced he had, and willed for the bottle on the table to move towards him. Epic fail. On the boy's final attempt, the pastor moved the bottle. The lesson I grasped from this scene was that we can only do so much in our own limited strength, but with help from a friend, or in fact our Father, we can do so much more. I was reminded of the importance of surrendering to God and asking Him, with His unlimited resources, for help in faith rather than going it alone. Let us never be convinced that we can rely on ourselves and need no one else. It is deception from the enemy.

Lesson 2: Touch lives during battle

The boy wanted his dad to return from XYZ—I wouldn't want to spoil the movie for you! The pastor gave the boy a list of selfless tasks to complete and explained that the boy's dad might return once the list was completed. Now, I don't necessarily agree with doing good to get good, or with the practise of bargaining with God. I don't serve an 'if I do this, God will do that' type of God. However, the beauty here is found in the list of selfless tasks that the boy attempts to perform. For example, the boy gave a patient a new comic book. I think we can agree this was a very sacrificial act, given he was under age eleven. The tasks the boy performed touched lives while he was battling to complete the list. His faith never wavered. Let's inconvenience ourselves at times to help others, even when we have nothing to gain.

Lesson 3: Don't drop your sword during battle

The boy had a vision of a version of the future, without his dad, which he chose not to accept. He continued to work for what he wanted despite what he saw or what others told him, and it worked in his favour. If our entire community, our family, friends, or colleagues, do not believe in our dream or what we desire, keep pressing despite what the eye can see. It's within reach if it's God plan; we know God is able and faithful to deliver.

Be encouraged to have faith, unwavering in nature, because this can move mountains.

Honesty Is the Best Policy

Have you ever been in a situation where you're facing a test and the best course of action is obvious, but you proceed to seek wise counsel anyway to reaffirm your options? It's almost as if we know what we should do, but we double-check in case our company thinks the other option, the wrong option, is a good one.

James 1:2-3 (NIV) says: "Consider it pure joy, my brothers and sisters, whenever you face trials of many kinds, because you know that the testing of your faith produces perseverance."

I was on mission in South Africa when I faced a test. The right thing to do should've been a no-brainer, given the fact that I was out there to be selfless. But I struggled with making the right decision. So what happened? What was the test?

I was at a diner for lunch, the type where the arrangement is one pays before being seated. I ordered some Greek salad and calamari with a can of Fanta. I thought the waitress behind the counter had heard my full order. I paid, and the change returned to me was more than I had expected to be given. Was I being blessed with a free can of Fanta, or had the waitress made a mistake and forgotten to charge me for the drink? Should I have drawn her attention to the fact that I had a free drink, or should I have kept quiet?

Have you ever faced this situation? What did you do? Was it on a small scale, like a free drink, or much bigger? What's the right thing to do here? I believe the way in which we deal with the small things in life reveals a lot about how we deal with the big things (Luke 16:10).

I turned to my company and sought guidance, as a battle was taking place in my mind. Why did I even ask? The thing about keeping good company is they tend to push you in the right direction. I was advised to inform the waitress of her mistake and pay for the drink, which is what I did. How many of us can seek wise counsel during such a moral dilemma? It's so important to be around the right people. Part of me was hoping the waitress would respond with "Oh, don't worry about it!" but that wasn't her reaction. Sometimes we can be so quick to be deceived that things are blessings when in fact we're meant to speak up, be honest and give it back.

Tests come in different forms, but honesty really is the best policy. The Bible says tests produce perseverance, and that perseverance produces character and character hope (Romans 5:3-4). Who doesn't want hope, eh?

Be encouraged to remain committed to doing the right thing.

What's in My Hand?

I bought a cup of tea from a cafe in the city. One brown sugar, enough milk, and I was good to go. It was so satisfying. But when I arrived at my desk, I noticed something. The ribbed packaging on the disposable tea cup was black and had started to turn my left hand black, mainly my fingers. The cup of tea was warm, but I never expected the colour to come off on my fingers. At that point I felt I had received a revelation.

Is the cup in our hands making our hands dirty? What is the cup? What's in the cup? It was only when I put the cup down that the colour began to fade from my fingers, and rightly so. Is there anything we need to put down? As enjoyable as the tea was, I did have to put down the cup, in this instance temporarily. Do we need a break from the cup or to throw it away altogether? Think. Reflect. Act.

I'm reminded of Matthew 5:29-30 (NIV), which says: "If your right eye causes you to stumble, gouge it out and throw it away. It is better for you to lose one part of your body than for your whole body to be thrown into Hell. And if your right hand causes you to stumble, cut it off and throw it away. It is better for you to lose one part of your body than for your whole body to go into Hell."

Now I'm not encouraging anyone to gouge out their eye or cut off their arm, but I would encourage a greater level of self-awareness, and circle awareness. We must love ourselves enough to do what's right for ourselves. There's often a battle in the mind when we evaluate the need for certain company or even projects we're undertaking. The responsibility to manage what we're carrying falls to us and us alone. We must be aware if these things are benefits or obstacles. As painful as temporary or permanent separation can be, if it's necessary, then there should be limited debate. The Lord was, is and always will be our strength.

Be encouraged to put cups down that need to be put down.

Finish What's on Your Plate
Before You Look for Dessert

Growing up, I'm sure it wasn't just my parents who overused the expression captured in the title above. "Finish what's on your plate before you look for dessert," they'd exclaim. But who really wants to eat the last bit of rice and vegetables, when chocolate gateau and apple crumble are waiting to be consumed? It's a hard battle to win, but we have to be disciplined.

Are we trying to have our next course before we've finished our current one? Are we trying to jump into the next season of life prematurely? Are we trying to move on to our next assignment without completing the one in front of us? God is a God of order, and we fool ourselves if we think we're ready ahead of schedule.

Every assignment we have needs to be completed before we can move on to the next one. If we go to tackle the next assignment early, we may very well find that we're unprepared and unqualified to complete it.

Ecclesiastes 3:1 (NIV) says: "There is a time for everything, and a season for every activity under the heavens." With this in mind, let's slow down and remain committed to what's in front of us. The irony is that by rushing or trying to skip a step, we end up working against ourselves. It almost becomes like running towards an open door but with each step taken, the corridor becomes longer and longer.

Additionally, we demonstrate disobedience by choosing our timeline over God's, which is sin. Let's not sin by rushing anything.

Be encouraged to eat every single green pea on your plate before reaching for the dessert spoon, because God is faithful to deliver on his promises. Dessert is coming.

WORKPLACE

Value Alignment

For nearly two years, I worked with a prestigious global firm where it was easy to get caught up in the perceived privilege and status. While I was fond of the BA flights and the four/five-star hotel lifestyle, it was hard not to fall victim to the usual workplace politics and being made to feel inferior during most meetings. This was worsened by frequent gossiping, cursing and backbiting. If it hadn't been for my convictions, I would've probably joined in with the rest. Instead, I rejected the culture but paid the price. I started to feel sad frequently and struggled under the pressures I faced.

After being off work for a few weeks due to stress, I was forced to stop, reflect and assess the situation. How was this happening to me? How was I allowing work to become so overwhelming? Where was God? Or had my eyes shifted to my troubles instead of being fixed on Him? I made affirming declarations of God's word over my life on a daily basis. You know, the popular ones: 'No weapon formed against me will prosper', 'Greater is He who is in me than He who is in the world'. Yet the situation remained seemingly unchanged.

After prayer and much reflection, I received great inner peace over the idea of resigning to restore my health. I had to let go of the social status attached to my job and the position I'd held. I felt true contentment once I did this, despite not having my next job lined up. I had to remain connected to God as my source of worth and trust in Him for security and provision. I had to make peace with the idea of not being able to afford the fine dining, spa breaks or monthly massages—oh how I miss them!

Letting go was the best decision I ever made, and my story even encouraged others to trust in God's ability to provide. I had time to heal, recalibrate and really think about my God-given purpose. I was strengthened by trusting in the Word, which says:

"Consider the ravens: they neither sow nor reap, they have neither storehouse nor barn and yet God feeds them. Of how much more value are you than the birds!" (Luke 12:24). God takes care of our needs before we even see them.

A new South African friend of mine really encouraged me when I told her I had resigned with no backup and a number of financial commitments. She said, "God knows best. No job or earthly thing can give you the inner peace you feel when you know you've made the right decision based on faith." I agreed 100 percent.

Sometimes we just need to take a risk and step out. The common phrase here is "step out into the unknown", but we must do this in faith, with prayer and God's wisdom. The safety net we have is the Lord; our confidence is rooted in His ability to provide. He's done it before and He'll do it again. We should always trust in Him—it's an exciting adventure when we do!

There's such a peace we feel when we completely surrender and run into the embrace of our Father. He's got the whole world in His hands—it's more than just a song. The safety net we have is the Lord, and our confidence is rooted in His sovereignty.

I found that if I couldn't operate in integrity and if the environment encouraged character change for the worst, then it didn't prove worth it. Even if offered a pay rise or more holiday, still it wouldn't be worth it. After all, what are we living for? Are we living for social status? For our own egos? Money? Cars?

Houses? Holidays? We live simply to glorify Him. Let's hold on to God's word as our basis for self-worth.

Be encouraged to trust Him enough to not compromise your identity, character or values in the workplace.

Featured on and edited by faithandvirtue.com

Breakthrough with the Simplest of Prayers

I expected it to be a usual day at work. One of those days where I knew exactly what was required of me. A 'get in, get out' type of day. My expectation was not met.

A senior colleague approached me just before lunch and asked me to complete a new task. Apparently my colleagues—yes, plural—had come down with a flu. How timely! The task was difficult in nature. It required extensive reading, followed by the production of a report in four parts. My appetite vanished. I was against the clock, so I buried my head in a number of printouts and got on with it. A quarter of the way through my reading, I began to feel somewhat overwhelmed. I didn't understand half of the financial terminology used and kept googling terms. I reread the assignment instructions, which had been captured in email, and felt like resigning instantly. A little childish perhaps, but I could and would have, though I'm so glad didn't. I was asking myself why I should stick around if I'd be set impossible tasks with limited support. Then I stopped.

I identified the thoughts to run away from the challenging task as a thought from the enemy. I made a conscious decision to ignore these thoughts and decided to mumble a quick prayer: "God, please help me get this done." That's when the strangest thing happened.

Psalm 17:6 (NIV) says: "I call on you, my God, for you will answer me; turn your ear to me and hear my prayer." Boy oh boy, can I testify to the Lord turning His ear to me and hearing my prayer.

So what happened? Well, within one hour, I'd finished parts one and two of the task. I still have no idea how, but it was like my mind was opened and I was able to get it done. I'm reminded of Hebrews 11:3 (NIV). which says: "By faith we understand that the universe was formed at God's command, so that what is seen was not made out of what was visible." Rather than seeing the task as too big and confusing, I logically broke it down into a number of smaller parts, and somehow was able to both find and understand the content. It's funny how we see clearer when we block certain thoughts, voices and influences, and when we humble ourselves and ask God for help. Food for thought.

I had complained about my day to family and friends when I reached home. But I was taught three lessons:

Lesson 1: God hears the simplest of prayers made by faith

Lesson 2: God never gives us more than we can handle

Lesson 3: God will meet us in our shortcomings

Let's continue to identify, isolate and disregard thoughts, voices and influences that are not of God.

Be encouraged to never belittle your ability, or convince yourself that you can't do anything. We're able to with the help of God.

Everything Has A Role

Have you ever eaten a plate of food with plastic cutlery, only for the fork to break? For a long time this puzzled me. I mean, I'd hate to think I was heavy-handed. I used to get two forks in preparation but realised it's so easy to have a backup plan, to prepare for the worst, to accept the mindset that the break of the fork isn't preventable.

I found that when I used the fork as a fork to scoop the food and not as a knife to cut the food, my fork wouldn't break as often. Solution: everything has a role. Consider the three points below:

Point 1: Prepare for the best

Why prepare for the worst when we can prepare for the best? Why get two forks when we can use one correctly and eliminate risk of breakage? If we put our efforts into effectively planning for the best outcome, rather than using all our energy towards preparing for the worst outcome, chances are things will work out, exceeding our expectations.

Point 2: Appropriate matching

Situations do not work favourably when we misuse resources. A fork isn't a knife. Sometimes there's a mismatch between the person and the task due to wanting to do it all. Let's not allow ourselves to become impatient, frustrated or short-tempered due to performing a task that was never even meant for us. Romans 12:6-8 encourages us to use our gifts appropriately. By doing so, order is sustained, and value is added in the workplace, and in our personal lives.

Point 3: Rely on others

No one can do it all. Why use a fork outside of its correct use when there are knives available? Why take on a role that wasn't meant for us at work when we have our own unique gifts, skills and abilities that God has blessed us with? We should be able to rely on others where we fall short skills-wise. Often our colleagues are there to fulfil roles that we can't perform adequately. Biblically, Christ gave different roles to equip his people for works of service, as described in Ephesians 4:11. I'd like to think our employers have the same strategy. It might be an inconvenience relying on another, and it could seem to be inefficient, but we cannot and are not supposed to do everything ourselves. There is great value in utilising our resources, teams and network to maximise our potential outputs and achievements.

Be encouraged to operate within your strengths, and to rely on others to fill the gaps. Work effectively.

Dismiss the Indirects

Sometimes our work ethic can offend our colleagues. It can be offensive to not be a slacker. It sometimes seems that, to work effectively, to be the first one in and last one out, to ensure all tasks are completed to a high standard, is deserving of penalisation.

Colossians 3:23 (NIV) says: "Whatever you do, work at it with all your heart, as working for the Lord, not for human masters." We are to work as if we're working for the Lord, and if we really were working for the Lord, we wouldn't slack. We would be punctual to work, we would give 150 percent to every task, and we would try our best to be blameless in the work setting.

Now I think we'd all agree that it isn't uncommon to sometimes get wind of negative whispers about ourselves, or to hear indirect comments made in our presence. These things can play on our minds for days, but it's important that we try our best not to take what others say about us to heart. We should confess and believe Acts 2:25 (NIV), which quotes David, saying: "Because he [the Lord] is at my right hand, I will not be shaken." When we know our life purpose, and when we have an unshakeable confidence in who we are, what our abilities are, and who we belong to, such comments should be like water off a duck's back. When we're blameless, it becomes obvious that the insecurity lies with those attempting to steal our peace and joy.

Luke 6:28 (NIV) says: "Bless those who curse you, pray for those who mistreat you." We are to pray for those colleagues who mistreat us, and bless those who speak negatively to us and over us. Let's be good to them, love them, and forgive them. Let's be sure not to let their indirect comments take root and negatively impact our perception of ourselves.

Be encouraged to continue to identify yourself with who God says you are. Stand on the Word of God, not the word of man.

Motives Aligned to Him

"Don't let who you were interfere with who God is allowing you to become"—commentary from the track "I forgive me" by James Fortune. It's easy to reflect on where we've come from and how we used to be a decade ago, two years ago, twelve months ago, or even last month, and feel guilt instead of gratitude. God saw it all, sees it all and still chooses us each and every day, according to 1 Peter 2:9.

In terms of the workplace, perhaps we used to go in each day, do the bare minimum as long as we were getting paid. But now we go into work diligently as if working for God rather than people. This was referenced in the previous encouragement titled "Dismiss the Indirects".

Perhaps before, we chose our company based on its reputation and the prestige associated with it in the hope of enhancing our status in society. But now we listen for God's perfect will and go where He sends us on assignment by faith, in obedience, and have an aim to be a light in a dark place, as described in John 1:5.

Maybe we used to be outspoken to demand a higher salary each year, and practised vocalising when we felt we weren't getting what we were worth. But now we have better wisdom on how and when we communicate such things, or we simply keep quiet and trust that God will move the heart of our employer to increase our salaries.

It's important to make sure our motives and behaviours are in line with what God expects; otherwise, we could be responsible for putting a wedge between ourselves and Him. It's important to keep pleasing God at the centre of everything we do.

Be encouraged to work as if God is your manager, to make sure your financial desires are kept in check, and that you don't get caught up chasing social status.

Reserve Criticism

Sitting in the cosy coffee area, I observed an employee pouring out her afternoon coffee. What bothered me was that she wasn't pouring the coffee into the large sink, which was clearly visible on her right, but rather into a drip tray.

I sat there, judging her in my heart, thinking this woman is so wicked. She's trying to flood the drip tray when the big sink is right there. For three days straight, for some reason, when I chose to eat my lunch at 12.30 p.m., she came at the same time shortly after to pour out her coffee.

It was the third time that a thought came to me to go look at what she was pouring her drink into. Oh my, I felt so bad! It turned out what I thought was a drip tray, which could get blocked, was a mini sink! I'm still thanking God that I didn't open my mouth to her. I learnt three key lessons from this:

Lessons 1: Reserve casting judgement

Sometimes we are fast to cast judgement and criticise what others are doing when it is us who need to change our perspective. Those we're focusing on could actually be innocent! This reminds me of Luke 6:37, which discourages judging others.

Lesson 2: Hold our tongues

Had I said anything, I would've looked like an idiot, and most likely would've caused great offence. Those of us who are passionate about standing up for injustice can probably relate, but we know the prudent hold their tongues, as captured in Proverbs 10:19.

Lesson 3: Repent to the Lord for the sins of the heart

The scripture says, in Proverbs 23:7 (NKJV): "For as a man thinks in his heart so is he..." To be brutally honest, I had wrongfully accused this woman—in my mind, anyway—and I despised an innocent person. Now this may sound harsh, but it's the truth. Just because I didn't act on it or say anything doesn't mean I didn't sin.

Be encouraged to be very careful with criticism, and to continue to seek the Lord's direction regarding when we should and shouldn't speak.

Ready. Aim. Fire.

Employment can be a challenge. Staying in good character can be difficult at work. While others fight to be popular, and compete for promotion, we might be more reserved and content with doing a great job. How do we cope when we feel we're being targeted because we behave against the majority?

I hear frequently of people being surrounded by negativity in the workplace both directly and indirectly. Numerous instances of bullying and harassment, resulting in one feeling victimised and miserable. On the bright side, we may recognise that we're growing in tolerance and patience while waiting on God to turn things around. But deep down, we're probably crying out to God for Him take the cup from us (Luke 22:42). Or has this only been my prayer in the past?

During one of my trying seasons, a friend reminded me of the fruit of the spirit 'long-suffering'. It's a painful one to experience, but it certainly does build character, and a reliance on God. But contrary to the title of this encouragement, do not retaliate. Do not get ready, take aim and fire at anyone who might be ill-treating you. If you're led to have a one-on-one meeting with those causing harm to your well-being, then do so. It's the polite way of turning tables over (Matthew 21:12, John 2:15, Mark 11:15). But it's important to stay in good character always.

A well-known Joyce Meyer expression is "if he [God] brings you to it, he [God] will bring you through it". Despite how it feels, as Christians, we trust the Bible scriptures that promise God will never put more on us than we can bear (1 Corinthians 10:13). Romans 8:31 reminds us that if our God is for us, then no one can be against us. We should remain empowered by the Holy Spirit which dwells in each of us (1 Corinthians 3:16).

Not fitting into the workplace can feel overwhelming, but we certainly have the necessary tools to endure these situations. May our eyes remain open to see the support God has arranged for us. Just like when Elisha asked the Lord to open his servant's eyes to see the angels who were on their side (2 Kings 6:16-17), I pray our eyes are opened to see that the support we have outweighs what's against us.

1 Peter 3:16-17 (NIV) reminds us that it's better to suffer for doing good than for doing evil, if it's Gods will. We go through challenging seasons, but that's what it is, a season. I pray we'll grow in wisdom on when to endure and when to move on.

Be encouraged to stay in good character in the workplace despite the storms we may experience.

TRANSFORMATION

He's Still Turning It Around!

Have you heard the expression 'I can feel someone is praying for me'? No? Well, I use it all the time. What does this statement mean, you may ask? When you find yourself in a situation where you can literally destroy someone verbally, and in your mind, they deserve it as they've been provoking you, but instead you choose to respond out of love. When you hear yourself, or read what you've written in response to someone, and you come to the realisation that you're changing or have changed for the better. I'm grateful that the Holy Spirit guards my tongue, and that rather than crushing someone, I choose to uplift them. You see, as a human being, it's normal to want to respond in an emotional way, but the Lord really does deal with each person in His timing so we don't have to.

Change Psalm 37:12-13 (KJV) says "The wicked plotteth against the just, and gnasheth upon him with his teeth. The Lord shall laugh at him: for He seeth that his day is coming."

Their day is coming! Be at peace. Let's allow God to fight our battles, and while he softens the hearts of those seeking to provoke us, let's be mindful of our communication. There's no need to get worked up.

I love how God is constantly working on the inside of us, and externally on those trying to provoke us via their words—even tone—or actions. I can personally testify to the fact that God is still in the business of turning situations around, ahead of us entering them. For example, I faced an issue with a tenant, but within forty-eight hours God turned it around a complete one-eighty. It went from potential eviction and hostile vibes to sharing a glass of red. Thankfully, the tenant displayed humility, and my communication was gentle when I sought to resolve the issue. The Lord said He would make our enemies our footstool, so let's be patient (Acts 2:35).

Be encouraged to keep praying for those around you, especially when you see their personality ills.

Oh, To Be Cleansed—'Soap And Water'

Is it ever right to bend the truth to keep the peace? Or to escape something? I wonder if it shows stronger character to just be bold and declare our truth despite the other person disagreeing. It's beautiful when our everyday communication reflects honesty. You know, when there's no deceit in order to gain anything from anyone, no cover-ups, and no exaggerations to be 'socially cooler'.

Psalm 141:3 (NIV) says: "Set a guard over my mouth, Lord; keep watch over the door of my lips."

Colossians 4:6 (NIV) says: "Let your conversation be always full of grace, seasoned with salt, so that you may know how to answer everyone."

It's important that we be very careful what we allow to leave our mouths, and tailor our communication to each person we speak to. Now I'm sure we've all told a few white lies in our time. A small slip of the tongue and all is forgotten. However, the Bible scriptures encourage us to guard our mouths and tongues to keep ourselves from calamity (Proverbs 21:23).

Calamity. How many times have we said something that's resulted in distress to ourselves or others?

I encourage us to ask God to search the depths of our hearts, to bring to light hidden or forgotten wrongs so we can be blameless in His sight, particularly in the area of speech. I pray we'll have people around us we can confess our sins to in the area of poor speech management. I pray we have people around us who can politely, and in a non-judgemental way, pull us up if we're guilty of poor speech management.

Be encouraged to take your time with your words.

Disobedience Déjà Vu

Have you ever experienced déjà vu? Of course you have, but have you ever experienced 'disobedience déjà vu'? Got you there, didn't I? Learning from mistakes isn't easy, but it's important that we make more effort in this area; otherwise, we can experience 'disobedience déjà vu'. Fancy reading about an example?

So it happened on a weekday morning. I was waiting for my usual bus into work, which would typically arrive at 8.07 a.m. On Mondays, the bus at that time is usually packed and drives right past my local bus stop, so it makes sense to walk to the stop before it. I knew this. Yet I wasn't standing at the stop before my local bus stop when the bus arrived. Right here is an example of facing a situation where I knew I should've done better but I didn't choose to do better. Let's call this a mistake.

Despite me mumbling, "Please stop, please stop," the bus drove right past. How many of us have been shown something to learn from, yet we haven't taken it on board? It's almost as if we don't trust our own previous experiences. It's like we're expecting the results to be different the second time round. Funnily enough, when I walked to the bus stop before my local one, I saw something I'd been hunting for—a free exercise park! I'd been looking for one for days but was too lazy to search on Google.

I'm a trendsetter. I didn't realise it before, but apparently I am. You see, I noticed I had a follower to the bus stop before my local one. I'm convinced that if I didn't walk to the stop before, no one else would have!

There were two lessons to be learned:

Lesson 1: When we learn from our mistakes and do things differently, the outcome is positive, but there's even more to gain. Sometimes things we didn't even know we could have, like a free exercise park, are discovered.

Lesson 2: When we learn from our mistakes, we lead the way for others to follow. We become a light to others who follow our example, like being a lamp unto their feet (Psalm 119:105).

Be encouraged to learn from mistakes, to take experiences on board for the future; otherwise, we might not survive our next 'flood'.

Angry Birds

I used to be so irritated when people would constantly invite me on Facebook to play Angry Birds, Candy Crush or Farmville. Can you relate? I'm thrilled that hype passed!

Another irritant of mine is public transport. Does it drive anyone else completely bonkers when you have evening plans and there are constant train delays and cancellations? It was a Friday evening when peace departed from my heart. I was absolutely livid! How could I miss a celebratory dinner held in honour of myself?

I was angry at the world, at trains, at the inventor of trains, at life, at family for not jumping at the suggestion to pick me up in their car, at myself for persisting with the impossible journey when I knew I wouldn't make it, and at God. Yes, at God. But why? I was angry at God because I knew deep down that He was working something out in my favour or for my protection (Romans 8:28). I was frustrated because I couldn't see what exactly He was up to. To tell you the truth, I didn't really care for it in that moment. You see, I had my plans. And I was hungry. Very hungry.

Proverbs 19:21 (NIV) says: "Many are the plans in a person's heart, but it is the Lord's purpose that prevails."

I should've been calm, but I wasn't. It took me three and half hours to get home. I still hadn't eaten. I was vexed! God's plan got me vexed! Immature or what? I'm not going to sugar-coat it. Due to the wrecked evening, I felt that a one-hour sulk was necessary. Like a child, I sulked. Well, I am a child; we're all children, children of the King. So, God and I had it out, and I almost got so real wanting a reaction, as we do, and all He told me was to rest in Him. It was like hitting someone, wanting them to hit you back, but instead they hug you. I didn't want Dad's hug. I deserved lightning. I was so confused. I didn't even want to know God in that moment; my flesh and my heart had failed, but He remained as my strength (Psalm 73:26).

It's a real relationship. The tantrum was real. But don't fight God, ever! He's always the winner! I realised it was wise to let go of my plans, to let go of myself and regain perspective.

Psalm 116:7 (NIV) says: "Return to your rest, my soul, for the Lord has been good to you." I clung to this verse. The Lord has always been good to me, so how dare I?

I wish I could testify about the goodness of God which was keeping me from food poisoning or an accident on the train, but the truth is, I still don't know why I missed my dinner. Does this frustrate you now as much as it frustrated me then?

I wonder, how do we deal with the disappointment of cancelled plans? Or when amazing opportunities come from nowhere and then are snatched away? Or when we're overlooked for promotion year after year when we know we're already performing at the level above? Or when after much self-work and prayer, we still seem to be experiencing failed relationship after relationship when we desire marriage? Or when we've been trying for years to fall pregnant, but the door just isn't opening? It's vital that we continue to trust God and submit to Him (Proverbs 3:5-6).

A wise lady reminded me that many want to have a physical six-pack but without the intense workout. Some situations are intense! But these situations are necessary to improve our attitudes when things go God's way and not ours. May the Lord continue to work on our collective attitudes when dealing with disappointment, in all areas of our lives (Daniel 11:35). The potter is still moulding us, and while the refining fires may be hot, they're necessary; we'll come out better than before (Isaiah 48:10, Proverbs 17:3).

Be encouraged to not be angry with God but instead appreciate His unpredictability.

It's Not Winter, Don't Add Layers

The gospel is simple. There isn't really a need to add layers to it. It amazes me somewhat when followers of Christ come up with blanket rules or theories that have no biblical support, or issue their own interpretation as definitive.

So how are layers added to the faith? Let's consider the two points below:

(1) What people should and shouldn't do

Some choices we make are personal to us due to our life experiences, struggles or even strengths. These shouldn't be put on others as if it's direction from the Lord Himself for every single believer. In some instances, people can be made to feel less of a Christian because they choose to do something or choose not to do something, and while neither option results in sin being committed, it's just not in line with what others would do. For example, regular prayer walks, spending X amount of time reading the Bible each week, frequency of fasting or even drinking alcohol. It can, in fact, be very discouraging to make opinionated statements that are delivered as facts in relation to the Christian walk.

(2) How people should be

It's a fine line to tread when advising others on how they should be. Yes, we should encourage each other and pray for each other's flaws. More often than not, people are aware of their improvement areas and don't need them to be called out regularly.

The fruits of the spirit are to be desired and demonstrated in our lives with the help of the Holy Spirit. Show me a human who can demonstrate all of these all of the time in all areas of their life, and I'll definitely try to touch the hem of their garment (Matthew 9:20). I love the expression 'slow and steady wins the race'. We need to be patient with ourselves and with others while our hearts are transformed and our behaviours are modified.

Be encouraged to be mindful not to add layers to this journey by making blanket statements based on our own opinions.

So Be Quiet

Have you ever been in a situation where someone throws pending pain or discomfort in your face and masks it as being informative? Or if someone reminds you of your current circumstance in a jokey way when you both know you're waiting for your circumstance to change?

2 Kings 2:3 (NIV) says: "The company of the prophets at Bethel came out to Elisha and asked, 'Do you know that the Lord is going to take your master from you today?' 'Yes, I know,' Elisha replied, 'so be quiet.'"

Elisha told the prophets to be quiet. Like Elisha, sometimes we need to silence unhelpful, unnecessary chatter. The chances are, if it isn't of an uplifting nature, it'll have the opposite effect.

Let's look at real-life examples of triggers and pressure points:

Example 1: You've been jobless for three months and someone jokes about you bumming around. But you know you've been actively looking for a new job.

Example 2: You've been single for a long season and someone makes a passing comment that you have no one, or they're curious about how you spend your Friday nights since you're single.

Example 3: You've been trying to save for something and someone enquires how much you have, to then reveal that it's much less than their expectation. This causes you to feel angry because they have no idea what you've been dealing with, or even if you've been supporting others. They don't know because they haven't bothered to ask.

Such queries aren't often genuine, and we need to use discernment. These comments leave the person's mouth to provoke our spirits to insecurity, fear, discouragement, even discontentment as we patiently wait for our breakthrough.

Let's be mindful that the enemy doesn't use our tongues to bring others down through the cover of humour or idle chat. Let's remain conscious speakers so we do not (un)knowingly or (un)intentionally let unhelpful talk leave our mouths. It's wise to challenge the thoughts and choice of words before they leave our mouths. I'm sure we all can relate as both the speaker of careless talk and the receiver. With wisdom, not malice or anger, we can address such talk and remain steadfast.

Be encouraged to stay secure and to not be shaken up in the face of provocative speech.

Heart of Thanksgiving

Do you have a heart of thanksgiving? How do you respond when you're given a gift? How do you respond when you're given a compliment? We should overflow with thankfulness.

Colossians 2:6-7 (NIV) says: "So then, just as you received Christ Jesus as Lord, continue to live your lives in Him, rooted and built up in Him, strengthened in the faith as you were taught, and overflowing with thankfulness."

While the context is to be thankful to the Lord, I'd like to focus on being thankful to others. We may be extremely grateful for something we've received or for something someone said, but our responses even in jest or banter may be interpreted as the opposite. When we receive a gift or a compliment, it's better to err on the side of caution and remain in line with social etiquette. It's wise to simply respond with a thank you. The reality is, some social norms are hardwired and not to be tampered with. I learnt this the hard way!

It's important that those gift or compliment givers feel valued as a result of their selfless actions and/or speech.

Be encouraged to overflow with thanksgiving.

Forgive Forgive Forgive

Do you struggle to forgive yourself? Or has someone ever done something to you that you believe is way beyond deserving your forgiveness? Do you doubt if even God would forgive you, or others? Consider the two points below.

Point 1: We should forgive ourselves—God has

Psalm 103:12 (NIV) says: "As far as the east is from the west, so far has he removed our transgressions from us."

We know God can and does forgive us irrespective of how badly we mess up.

I can't even begin to measure the distance between the east and the west, but that distance according to Bible scripture is how far God has removed our sins from us. Great news! We don't need to live feeling weighted down by our past mistakes. We don't need to feel condemned. We know Jesus didn't come to condemn the world but rather to save the world through Him (John 3:17), to reconcile us to our God. We should accept that we are forgiven.

God is merciful to our unrighteousness and wickedness, and He chooses to forget our sins (Hebrews 8:12). His mercies are new every morning (Lamentations 3:22-23) and He has compassion on us time and time again, so much so that He casts all our sins into the depths of the sea (Micah 7:19).

Point 2: We should forgive others, ask God to forgive those who have wronged us

I find it easier to forgive myself but more of a challenge to forgive others. When I'm wronged, it can take a long while before I've genuinely forgiven the person. It's a dangerous space to be in because it can result in resentment. I'd love to reach a place where I can forgive someone at the point of offence.

Matthew 6:14-15 (NIV) says: "For if you forgive other people when they sin against you, your Heavenly Father will also forgive you. But if you do not forgive others their sins, your Father will not forgive your sins." I wonder if, like me, you need to forgive people quicker.

We should even ask God to forgive those who offend us. In Acts 7:59-60, we see that Stephen asked the Lord to forgive those who were stoning him. In Luke 23:34, we hear Jesus asked the Father to forgive us in our ignorance. I commend anyone who's actively asking God to forgive those who have wronged them; I know this isn't something I do regularly.

I love Colossians 3:13 (NIV), which says: "Bear with each other and forgive one another if any of you has a grievance against someone. Forgive as the Lord forgave you." The reality is, none of us is perfect, so we need to be very cautious that we don't fall into the trap of harbouring unforgiveness.

Be encouraged to ask God for forgiveness, but also to walk in the knowledge that you are forgiven.

PROVISION

Modern-Day A Bug's Life

Are you afraid of anecdotes about ants? If yes, please skip over this page. Okay, I warned you!

I was sitting in my parents' back garden and I stepped on an ant, on purpose. While I recognise this to be murder in cold blood (Exodus 20:13), or Grievous Bodily Harm (GBH), it was purely instinct, despite the ant being in its natural habitat. Post-criminal activity and post-death—rest in peace, Anty—an interesting course of events took place.

Part 1:

Unexpectedly, another ant came to the deceased's rescue. As I bent down to observe what was happening, I could see the energetic ant circling the corpse frantically. I guess it was a relative? Sorry again! But the ant tried to put the corpse on its back and was failing. Then out of nowhere, another ant came to help, and they were carrying the corpse on their backs! Well, the second ant, the helper, was pushing the corpse with its head onto the back of the relative. I was very afraid of their intelligence at that point, but what came to mind was that sometimes we all just need some help, and often there are people willing to help if we open our eyes to see and receive the support. This reminds me of Galatians 6:2, which encourages us to carry each other's burdens.

Part 2:

The ants were on a mission from the pavement to the grass, but one was moving faster than the other and then... yes, you guessed it! They dropped the corpse! I was thinking, *God, are you being serious? After showing me the provision of a helper ant, and the great teamwork between the two, are these ants really going to fail their mission?* But before I could even finish my thought, wind blew the corpse to the grass! Very timely. Then the duo headed to the grass.

How is it possible that when we need extra help, God shows up? When our resource is exhausted, God remains faithful and provides others to support us. When the joint effort fails, he steps in and supernaturally coordinates circumstances to work in our favour. Hebrews 6:10 (NIV) says: "God is not unjust; He will not forget your work and the love you have shown Him as you have helped His people and continue to help them."

Be encouraged to continue to believe that God will intervene supernaturally, and to not step on ants in their natural habitat.

He Alone Remains Able and Willing

Do you believe God is both able and willing? Do you believe He's in your corner?

Isaiah 51:10 (NIV) says: "Was it not you who dried up the sea, the waters of the great deep, who made a road in the depths of the sea so that the redeemed might cross over?"

In this scripture, we hear Isaiah remembering the power of the Lord. God is powerful; He is able and He is willing. God protects us, and wants only the best for us. He always comes through. Always!

Sometimes we need to reflect on where God has brought us from and give thanks for where we currently are. We can't afford to forget the journey or His role in that journey. This is what gives us the confidence to continue. If we make a conscious effort to remember what He's done for us, we wouldn't think to doubt His ability, His willingness or His intention in our lives.

We serve a God who parted the sea! That's a door I'm sure the Israelites were grateful God closed. Moreover, we serve a God who raised Jesus Christ from the dead. I'm sure we're all grateful for this! I love that our God is never changing, and He doesn't fail us. Psalm 121:3 reassures us that God is very much awake and at work in our lives.

It must be reiterated that our God is not dead, so let's lean into Him, trust Him, and love Him wholeheartedly. Remember where He's brought us from and that He's still with us now. If He chooses to close a door, it's for our benefit.

Be encouraged to remember who God is and what He's capable of. Remember His presence in your journey, His hand on your life. Do not doubt His ability or good intentions towards you.

Already Redeemed

Do you ever get caught in the trap where you think you need to be doing a lot more for God? It's a tricky one because the Word of God talks about storing up treasures in heaven (Matthew 6:19-20) and doing good deeds (1 Timothy 6:18), while the gospel in its simplest and purist form is that we're saved by grace through faith (Ephesians 2:8-9), and are moulded into God's likeness (Romans 12:2). God provided his son's blood as our ransom, so good deeds will not buy us our salvation—it was already purchased.

Titus 3:5-6 (NIV) says: "He saved us, not because of righteous things we had done, but because of His mercy. He saved us through the washing of rebirth and renewal by the Holy Spirit, whom He poured out on us generously through Jesus Christ our Saviour."

There are two key areas for exploration:

Area 1: Good deeds or not, we're still redeemed:

We have nothing to prove to anyone; our good works aren't what gets us through heaven's gates. Hebrews 10:24 encourages us to consider how we can push each other towards good deeds. At the same time, we need to be mindful to strike a good balance in our lives and make sure we don't take on too much. For example, attending two services every Sunday, prayer meetings, Bible study and connect groups in the week, as well as volunteering on a team or two on top of working every day, maintaining a home and looking after a family leaves little room for rest. We should continue to pursue a personal relationship with the Lord rather than religious activities.

The Bible scriptures instruct us to continue to gather (Hebrews 10:25), but let's not get carried away and take on so many commitments that it leaves us exhausted. Sometimes we put undue pressure on ourselves, particularly spiritually, and this shouldn't be so. Yes, we should read our Bibles, have a prayer life, give time to worship, belong to a church and serve where possible, but we aren't less in the eyes of God if we don't do it all, all the time.

Area 2: When we fail tests, we're still redeemed:

To the born-again, tests will inevitably come our way, and if we don't pass the first time, we shouldn't beat ourselves up. I've heard the enemy whisper some nonsense after failing a test or two or three. Lies like I'd be automatically Hell-bound, or that I should feel guilty, or that I should redeem myself through good deeds.

Our walk is spirit-led, not self-led. I'm not encouraging complacency. I'm addressing the mindset that could lead to us burning out and/or feeling guilty. We're loved and accepted by the Lord.

Be encouraged to embrace the truth of the gospel, and take the spiritual journey one day at a time.

Our Steps Are Ordered

Are you single and feeling anxious? Are you doubting if Mr or Mrs Right will ever appear in your life? Don't panic and don't embrace fear, because your steps are ordered.

Psalm 37:23 (NKJV) says: "The steps of a good man are ordered by the Lord, and he delights in his way."

The one the Lord has for each of us, we will never have to question. God is purposeful. His grace is indescribable, so continue to trust Him. When it's your time, you will know, and it'll be till death do you part. Enjoy the season you're in. Wake up, do what you like when you like. Eat cereal for dinner and leftover dinner for breakfast carefree. No him making her dinner each evening or her making for him. Book a flight leaving next week. Splash out on a new pair of trainers, guys, or wedges, ladies. Get that mortgage money together. Clear that credit card. Take that salsa class. Learn that language.

Provision has been made from when you were in your mum's womb. You are chosen, you are not forgotten, you are not forsaken. You are amazing! You are handsome. You are beautiful (Psalm 139:14). You are who God says you are. Let your confidence remain. Don't let the season unsettle you. Stay seated. Son of the King. Daughter of the King. Rest and watch your stories unfold.

Proverbs 3:5 (NIV) says: "Trust in the Lord with all your heart and lean not on your own understanding." So, continue to trust God and His timing.

She will be supportive of him (Genesis 2:18), a mentor for other women (Titus 2:4-5), worthy of respect (1 Timothy 3:11), selfless (Proverbs 31:20). He will be intentional or else silent, a leader (1 Corinthians 11:3, Ephesians 5:23), provider (1 Timothy 5:8), prayerful (1 Timothy 2:8), disciplined (1 Timothy 3:4), ready to leave his family to join her (Genesis 2:24).

You will look back in gratitude as you taste of our Father's goodness, kindness, faithfulness.

Be encouraged to enjoy Father-son time, Daddy-daughter time, and give God thanks in advance.

Delay Is Our Protection

During my partial kitchen refurbishment, the opportunity presented itself to cut corners. In short, the gas engineer offered to fit an electric hob. Fortunately, the electric hob didn't arrive on time. Unfortunately, this meant I'd have to pay an additional fee for an electrical engineer to perform the installation when the gas engineer could've done it for free in less than ten minutes. Or so I thought!

Lesson 1: Never let an unregistered person carry out an installation in your home

In the Christian faith, our bodies are referred to as temples. We are spirit in body; our body is the home of our spirit, a temple for the Holy Spirit (1 Corinthians 6:19). Let's be careful here, as some unregistered individuals may want to refurbish our temple. Be on guard and exercise both wisdom and discernment, because not every modification is suitable for the home of your spirit (1 Corinthians 10:23).

Lesson 2: Do not cut corners when refurbishing

I wanted to cut corners and let the gas engineer act like an electrician in order to get the job done quickly. But there really is no need to rush. There are no shortcuts to refurbishing your temple. Exercise patience because it takes time, energy, sacrifice, and continuously giving up the old self to see beneficial changes to our temple. Do not sow sparingly (2 Corinthians 9:6). Commitment to prayer, fasting, studying the Bible, accountability, godly community and fellowship are required. Be patient with self and refurbishments will take place, sometimes without you even realising.

Lesson 3: Look ahead for support

The first engineer had completed his job and should not have been allowed to perform the second job. In our spiritual journey, we go through seasons. Those who helped to refurbish our temple in the last season might not be the most appropriate individuals to support our refurbishments in the present or next season. Sometimes we look back to these individuals rather than ahead to who God has positioned around us. Let's not forget Lot's wife (Genesis 19:26). Let's keep your gaze ahead (Proverbs 4:25-27).

Lesson 4: Delay is our protection

I was extremely grateful for the delayed arrival of the electric hob. It was for my protection, because the installation took a couple of hours, which revealed to me that the gas engineer wouldn't have been able to perform the complex job. Our delay is for our protection from ourselves, our desires, as well as protection from others. Let's trust in God always (Proverbs 3:5-6).

Be encouraged that our Lord and Saviour is not slow to fulfil His promises to us (2 Peter 3:9). He is always on time, so let's wait patiently for positive change.

Learn to Receive

I don't know about you, but I have a hard time receiving. What can I say, I'm a giver! Acts 20:35 (NIV) reveals to us that it's better to give than to receive. When your parents raise you with the mentality of 'owe no man anything', it becomes so easy to misunderstand and extend this to 'accept nothing from anyone'.

It was only during a season of financial instability when I realised I had to change. I was offered financial help, but like always, I was in the habit of declining the offer. I was of the mindset that I would rather not take anything from anyone. But by being of that mentality, I was robbing others of having the opportunity to be 'blessed for being a blessing'.

I realised it was a challenge for me to receive due to two reasons.

Reason 1: Pride

Sometimes the enemy will deceive us into thinking we're doing the right thing when in fact we're not. Humility comes in many different forms, and if Proverbs 22:4 is correct that the reward for humility and fear of the Lord is riches and honour and life, which it obviously is, then there's a need for reflection in this area. For me, it was time to let my strong persona take a rest.

Reason 2: Not wanting to be a burden to others

We shouldn't feel as if we're burdening others if we're making a prayer request, needing a shoulder to lean on during a rough time, or in my case, if someone has offered to help financially. In Exodus 17, we see Aaron and Hur provided Moses with a stone to sit on when he grew tired. They even held his hands up so the Israelites would defeat the Amalekites in battle.

Be encouraged to support each other and to in turn accept support. Be willing to give and to receive.

Raise the Bar

Do you take time to appreciate God each day? Do you wake up with an expectation that He'll reveal himself to you in one way or another? God loves to commune with us through fellowship with the Holy Spirit (2 Corinthians 13:14), and as He is surely with us, we should be able to see Him at work.

1 Corinthians 2:9 (KJV) says: "But as it is written, eye hath not seen, nor ear heard, neither have entered into the heart of man, the things which God hath prepared for them that love Him."

While this scripture is a pleasant reminder that God has prepared mind-blowing and unimaginable things for those who love Him, these things are often considered to be big in size rather than small.

I experienced a small, generous gesture. It was so unexpected. I was taking the train home in an overcrowded carriage. The type of scene where there's hip contact with strangers and faces are in armpits. Grim, right? I'm sure we've all been there. At the time, I was completely exhausted from a mentally demanding day. There was nowhere to sit, so I found contentment in standing, as awkward as it was.

The train arrived at the next stop and a lady got off. She'd been standing in a corner, leant up against it. I thought, *Great, I'll take that spot!* But at that same moment, two people who were sitting down rushed off the train. It was a little strange!

There was no visibility of interest in the seats from any passengers at all, so I sat down and enjoyed the ride.

How was it that I was content to stand, then content to stand leant against a corner, but then suddenly, seats were available. I love it when the Lord provides in an unexpected way.

Now evidently, this is a very small blessing. Am I expressing gratitude over a simple seat? Yes, I am! What dawned on me, during that moment, was that when we're content in life, the Lord may bless us to better our circumstance. Better still, sometimes the blessing is greater than what we immediately see.

I learnt to raise the bar of expectation. God is good. Eyes have not seen, and ears have not heard! We most likely are familiar with Jeremiah 29:11, and Ephesians 3:20, but do we really believe it? We should!

When we see God in the little things and give Him thanks, we'll definitely see Him in the big things and continue to give Him thanks. May our eyes remain open to see the small everyday blessings.

Be encouraged to raise the bar of expectation when it comes to God.

Idolatry Be Gone

Have you ever accidentally tripped over an item on the floor? What about putting the item in your own path to then trip over it? It wouldn't make sense to do that, right? But we can become our own stumbling block if we don't accept our passenger seat in the vehicle of life with our Lord as the driver. If God is the driver, we should trust Him to get us from A to B, even if a storm hits us, causing extreme anxiety (1 Peter 5:7).

During my season of singleness, I strengthened my personal relationship with the Lord, but during chaotic times, I realised He wasn't always my go-to. How could it be that He was the driver of my life, yet I desired another male figure in His place to be a rescuer?

It was a Thursday afternoon, and I was tolerating an overbearing colleague. I was left with no other choice but to retreat to an empty meeting room in order to pray. Had I not chosen to do this, I probably would've destroyed him verbally. Thank God for wisdom, eh? It was 11:00 a.m., and I already felt so exhausted. I wanted to share the burden with someone, with a companion, with a life partner, but no one was there. I looked at the contact list in my phone as if a number would suddenly appear. How sad, right? But it happens!

Psalm 46:1 (NIV) says: "God is our refuge and strength, an ever-present help in trouble."

Therefore, I prayed. I needed my Heavenly Father to rescue me. My prayer was simple and honest in nature: "God, if only

I had a man to receive encouragement from right now." The Lord replied to me: "No man is your Saviour. I am." In that moment, I started thanking God for being my helper in this time of trouble. I felt so much better!

But in that instance, the Lord revealed something key to me. He revealed to me that if I had a life companion, I would've placed him above God. I would even go as far as saying I would've replaced God as the first point of contact. It was a moment of revelation. My Heavenly Father didn't want to lose His place as centre of my life to any man. God is a jealous God (Exodus 34:14), and He certainly knows best. He wouldn't provide a God-fearing companion until He knew for sure that He would remain centre of my life. It's so important to make a conscious effort to maintain our personal relationships with the Lord. Always confide in Him first, even when a life companion is there.

Be encouraged to carefully examine if there is an idol in your life, and don't stand in your own way to victory by looking for solutions outside of our Lord.

BONUS LETTERS

Father's Love Letter

Dear Beloved Child,

This is your Heavenly Father. There is no time like the present for me to express to you how much I adore you.

I love you so much that I gave my only begotten son to die for you (John 3:16). Continue to show this love to others in your sphere of influence (1 John 4:11). Do not love with word or speech, but with actions and truth as I do for you (1 John 3:16-18).

Do everything with love (1 Corinthians 16:14). Do everything with me, for I am love (1 John 4:8). The depths of my love for you are boundless. While you were intentionally sinning, my son died for you (Romans 5:8). You are so very worth it; you are worth every blood drop that was shed (Matthew 26:28).

Do continue to love me with all your heart, soul and mind (Mark 12:30). Continue to cry out to me, as my unfailing love will always support you (Psalm 94:18-19). I will provide for every one of your needs (Philippians 4:19), so don't doubt. You may suffer through a season (2 Corinthians 1:5, 1 Peter 4:13) where you are going through a refining fire, or when you are receiving my discipline, but I will never abandon you (Acts 2:27).

Love from Dad.

Dear Comparison

Dear Comparison,

Please leave us alone. Time and time again, you creep up on us, in our quiet moments, in our own personal reflective time, in the form of negative self-talk.

We might indulge in you regrettably, but no more. Who he is or who she is and what they have or do is completely okay with us. We're confident in our own skin, in our own walk in life, and we choose to behave fuelled by our own drive rather than because of any envy of others. Philippians 2:3 says: "Do nothing from rivalry or conceit, but in humility count others more significant than yourselves." So don't even try to play the rivalry card with us!

We accept that our time schedule in all areas of life is different from other people's. Our achievements will vary; we might gain material possessions, or amazing life experiences, or we might not. James 1:17 says: "Every good gift and every perfect gift is from above, coming down from the Father of lights with whom there is no variation or shadow due to change." So if God doesn't want to give us something right now, or at all, we're fine with that as He knows best. We trust in God's tailored provision.

Galatians 2:20 says: "I have been crucified with Christ. It is no longer I who live, but Christ who lives in me. And the life I now live in the flesh I live by faith in the Son of God, who loved me and gave Himself for me." Comparison, stop trying to turn our eyes onto ourselves when we need to keep our eyes fixed above.

Our flaws might seem greater than others', but the truth is we never know the reality versus the pretence. Yes, there are things we're working on in our lives, and we refuse to believe that others don't also have areas for improvement.

Comparison, you will not take hold of our hearts or our minds. We will make a conscious effort to not give you time in our twenty-four-hour day—yes, including when we rest at night and dream.

Comparison, you are an obstacle to contentment in Christ. We will not lose sight of our own blessings. We will be thankful for who we are and what we have rather than focusing on what we lack, for where we are weak, our God is eternally strong. We make a decision today to not entertain you but instead to invest our time and thoughts wisely in strengthening our position in life. If you do decide to return despite being unwelcome, may God open our ears to recognise your awful voice in our minds. And may we boldly exclaim, "Shut up and goodbye."

Signed,
Us believers.

As featured on faithandvirtue.com

Special thanks to Hot Tree Editing for the professional service they consistently provide to new authors.
https://www.hottreeediting.com/

Ingram Content Group UK Ltd.
Milton Keynes UK
UKHW012201200323
418888UK00013B/332/J